How to . . .

get the most from your

COLES NOTES

Key Point

Basic concepts in point form.

Close Up

Additional hints, notes, tips or background information.

Watch Out!

Areas where problems frequently occur.

Quick Tip

Concise ideas to help you learn what you need to know.

Remember This!

Essential material for mastery of the topic.

Your guide to...

Separation & Divorce

- Legal process
- Custody & access
- Division of property

COLES NOTES have been an indispensable aid to students on five continents since 1948.

COLES NOTES now offer titles on a wide range of general interest topics as well as traditional academic subject areas and individual literary works. All COLES NOTES are written by experts in their fields and reviewed for accuracy by independent authorities and the Coles Editorial Board.

COLES NOTES provide clear, concise explanations of their subject areas. Proper use of COLES NOTES will result in a broader understanding of the topic being studied. For academic subjects, COLES NOTES are an invaluable aid for study, review and exam preparation. For literary works, COLES NOTES provide interesting interpretations and evaluations which supplement the text but are not intended as a substitute for reading the text itself. Use of the NOTES will serve not only to clarify the material being studied, but should enhance the reader's enjoyment of the topic.

© Copyright 2001 and Published by
COLES PUBLISHING. A division of Prospero Books
Toronto – Canada
Printed in Canada

Cataloguing in Publication Data
Sharkey, John, 1943–

Your guide to ... separation and divorce : legal process,
custody & access, division of property

(Coles notes)
Written by John Sharkey
Includes bibliographical references. ISBN 0-7740-0641-2

1. Divorce – Law and legislation – Canada – Popular works.
2. Separation (Law) – Canada – Popular works.
I. Title. II. Title: Separation & divorce. III. Series.

KE569.2.S52 2001   346.7101'66   C2001-930444-7
KF535.S52 2001

Publisher: Nigel Berrisford
Editing: Paul Kropp Communications
Book design: Karen Petherick, Markham, Ontario
Layout: Richard Hunt

Cover photo: Digital Imagery® copyright 1999 PhotoDisc, Inc.

Manufactured by Webcom Limited
Cover finish: Webcom's Exclusive DURACOAT

Contents

Chapter One

Divorce - Are you sure?

At its easiest, divorce is a legal and emotional undertaking that somehow has to be endured before you and your partner can move on to a new life. At its worst, divorce can be a devastating battleground wreaking havoc on every member of your family, especially children. Although this book concentrates on the legal aspects of divorce, the emotional, economic and parenting disruptions of marriage breakdown are always more significant.

Some social scientists have attempted to understand the divorce process by breaking it down into roughly three areas: the emotional crisis, the economic crises and the parenting crisis. These areas are complex and interwoven and obviously vary from individual to individual and situation to situation. Nevertheless, here's what you can expect after you and your partner decide to split up.

THE EMOTIONAL ISSUES

The emotional stress of separation and divorce is a universal reality. To varying degrees, both you and your partner will experience a deep personal loss and – after the breakup – a real sense of isolation. Moreover, the emotional upheaval of a divorce affects everyone within the family, particularly children and close relatives such as grandparents.

Divorce also affects you in other ways. For instance, it is common for people going through the divorce process to resort to compulsive behaviors such as eating or drinking too much or drug abuse. Some become despondent or hyperactive. Some throw themselves into their work or into super-parenting to avoid dealing with their difficulties. None of these is healthy in dealing with a breakup.

Some family specialists have compared the emotional stages a person goes through while separating to the experience of people approaching death: there are similar stages of denial, anger, bargaining, depression and acceptance. Both spouses can experience these different emotions although a spouse who doesn't want the divorce probably experiences them more severely than a spouse who wants to leave the relationship.

Denial "Don't worry, you'll get over it." This a common reaction to a spouse's discontent and the possibility of divorce, especially for people who have been married a long time. Our identity can be heavily wrapped up in our marriage and any threat to it is a deep threat to our sense of security and well-being. Often a person just denies that anything is wrong with the marriage. It's easier to blame a discussion of separation on a partner's work or depression and then speak confidently of things getting back to normal with time. Sometimes relationships improve after a crisis, but most often they do not.

Anger "You're ruining my life!" This stage often arrives when one partner is forced to face the fact that the other wants out. One or the other has moved out – not for an angry night, but for a week or more. A lawyer's letter arrives and there is no denying the situation any longer. You may react with anger at the departing spouse, other family members or too often at yourself. It is usually at this point that you hire a lawyer and carry out your angry feelings through legal proceedings. Decisions made during this phase are often only meant to punish the other spouse and may well lead to regret later when your new life is established. Remember, anger always leads to needless lawyer's fees.

Bargaining "Let's give it another chance... I'll make it up to you!" This is usually a desperate attempt to postpone the inevitable. Denial is over, anger has perhaps subsided, but now one of you begins to make promises, often unrealistic. A spouse may promise to be more communicative or to right the wrongs that they know are present in the relationship. Another may promise to give up a lover or to be a better parent. Only you can judge if such bargaining yields a real bargain.

Depression "My life is ruined!" In this phase, you both have to face reality and you will not like much of what you see. You begin to become aware of what you are losing. You come to realize the benefits of the family relationship and your own fear of the future. A psychologist can sometimes help you deal with this phase and the regret and guilt that accompany it.

Acceptance "All right, now what?" At this emotional stage of the divorce, you are ready to accept the reality of the breakup and are prepared to move on. You begin to see a light at the end of the tunnel, to see new romantic and personal possibilities, and you're prepared to plan for the future. To do this properly, the details of the old relationship need to be tied up and left behind as much as possible.

 Dealing with these stressful emotional stages requires the passage of time. Unfortunately, people are often forced to make long-lasting legal and parenting decisions while they are in the midst of emotional upheavals. Take your time, get advice from family and friends, and hire a good lawyer.

THE ECONOMIC ISSUES

Whatever the bonds of love and family, marriage is also an economic relationship. Over time, married couples gain property and create wealth. When it comes time to separate, it is also time to divide the material property and split the wealth. This, too, can be gut-wrenching.

Both partners in a relationship suffer financially and are worse off alone than when they were together. Two people, especially with children, living apart cannot live as cheaply as in one household. If you are a single mother with children or a middle-aged homemaker with few marketable skills, you are going to suffer more than your husband who has a high income, but usually both spouses will experience a drop in real income. Even when a husband pays support payments in full and on time, the wife or the wife and children are rarely able to maintain the same standard of living as when the family was together. Sadly, many women and children end up living at or below the poverty line.

Unfortunately, many support payers (mostly men) do not fully honor their support obligations. This forces many women to depend on their own jobs or social assistance to meet the needs of their families, because no provincial program of support collection, wage garnishees or driver's licence revocation can guarantee that a support cheque will arrive on time.

PARENTING ISSUES

Although a disintegrating relationship affects the two spouses most immediately, the long-term effects are often felt by the children. Adults may be traumatized by the split-up, but they often get over their pain within a year or two. Children are more deeply affected and for a longer period of time, sometimes for the rest of their lives.

Children tend to see the world very much through their own eyes. When they realize their parents are splitting up, their world is severely disrupted. Their idealized view of parents is shattered and serious behavioral problems can result. It is common for young children to act out their unhappiness by getting low marks, having tantrums or becoming depressed. Most tragic of all is that children often imagine they are to blame for the breakup of their parents. Since you, as parents, will be going through a difficult emotional time yourselves, you will be hard-pressed to provide the emotional support that your children need during this difficult time.

It is especially important to provide children of all ages with support during a relationship breakup. Kids need different kinds of support at different ages but they all need attention, even grown children who have left home. If resources are not available for professional support, grandparents or other close family members can provide a much-needed sense of continuity and stability during these difficult times.

MARRIAGE COUNSELLING

If you and your partner can agree to do so, it is useful to consult with a marriage counsellor. There is nothing to lose and everything to gain. Counsellors are professionals trained to help you come to a realistic understanding of the dynamics of your relationship. Often they will be able to help you understand the strengths and weaknesses of the marriage and may help you and your spouse reconcile. On the other hand, if they come to believe that the relationship is beyond help, they will assist you to develop approaches that will make the separation easier.

Case study: Robert and Yvette

Robert and Yvette had been married for 12 years when the crisis hit. They married shortly after graduating from university, and have two children, a 10-year-old boy and an eight-year-old girl, and lived in a charming but heavily mortgaged suburban house. As a couple, Robert and Yvette were very loving, if not terrifically passionate, and thrilled with each other's successes, until the twelfth year.

The problems in their marriage had no specific cause – no affair, no sudden shift in goals, no family crisis. Yet the problems had been mounting. Yvette's mother had died and Yvette was increasingly concerned about her father, who was living alone in a small town in Quebec. Robert's accounting career had taken him into management, so suddenly he was working nights, travelling on weekends and too tired to be much of a father or a husband. Yvette, too, was exhausted, feeling that a full-time job in a hospital and a full-time job as a parent were too much for her without Robert's help. Given the growing emotional distance between them, separation began to look attractive.

It was the prospect of telling the children – especially their daughter, Megan – that sent the couple to counselling rather than to divorce court. If they did divorce, Robert would likely move out, Yvette would have to give up the house, the children's lives would be massively disrupted, the lawyers would pick up thousands of dollars ... but would Robert and Yvette be happier?

After three months of counselling, they decided against splitting up. They shared a great deal besides the children: history, goals, religion, friends, family, even some remnants of love. Their relationship had reached a crisis but not a breaking point. With some accommodation by each of them, the immediate problems were resolved. Robert and Yvette are still married, 10 years later, and very glad that their crisis did not result in a breakup.

Chapter Two

Going to a lawyer

HIRING A LAWYER

Before you hire a lawyer to take your case, there are a number of points you should bear in mind. First, always remember that the lawyer is *for* you. You are spending your hard-earned money for someone to represent your interests as you see them.

Because divorce is difficult emotionally, it is wise to choose a lawyer in whom you have confidence. You need someone who will give you the best advice, even if you may not like hearing it. This could save you time, energy and money in the long run.

Never use the same lawyer as your spouse no matter how well you are getting along. Often spouses approach the family's lawyer, the one they have been dealing with on other matters such as real estate, to handle their divorce. A good lawyer will not take on both of you. In a split-up both parties have different interests, so they must have two different lawyers representing them.

At all costs, avoid lawyers who are eager to go to court, trying to convince you they can get a large settlement. An aggressive lawyer and an angry partner are a recipe for prolonged litigation and an unsatisfactory settlement. Settlements that are not close to being mutually agreeable are prone to failure, becoming a source of continued hostilities between former spouses. Even if the legal aspects of the divorce are settled, there is still opportunity for continuing hostilities through the children. A classic dynamic is that dad doesn't make full support payments, so mom withholds parenting opportunities for dad – or vice versa. Both parties are in breach of their agreements and the law, but the real losers are the children.

Although there is no ideal lawyer, you should be looking for someone whom you feel comfortable with. You need someone who is experienced in family law, who listens to what you say and who might also say things to you about your case that you may not want to hear.

You can ask your friends for references and most provinces have special referral services that you can locate by contacting your provincial law society. For instance, the Ontario Law Society has organized lawyers by professional specialization. This does not necessarily mean that the lawyers have any specialized training in this type of law, but it does mean that they have experience in that field.

It is a good idea to make a short list of two or three perspective lawyers and then go and make an appointment to interview them. Most lawyers give a free half-hour consultation. This gives you the opportunity to see whether they are a good match for you. Go prepared with a detailed history of your marriage and what has happened to date.

Depending on the complexities of your divorce or separation, you should inquire whether the lawyer you are interviewing will be the person handling your case. Much of the work in a straightforward case can be taken on by junior lawyers or competent legal secretaries. However, you want to be assured the lawyer you hire will be doing the serious legal and court work.

Most provincial law societies have a lawyer referral service. For a minimal fee ($6 in Ontario) you can get a free half-hour consultation. If you like the lawyer you can hire them or try someone else. Provincial law societies also have a list of their members. To locate your provincial law society, look under law society in the white pages of your phone book. If you have access to the Internet go to the excellent Web sites like **www.lawnet.com** or **www.canlaw.com** which will provide you with links to all the law societies' Web pages.

Confidentiality One of the most important aspects of the lawyer-client relationship is the issue of confidentiality. For a lawyer to work in your best interests, he or she needs to know everything about your case. That means knowing a lot about you. In order to do this you must feel assured that whatever you say to a lawyer is kept in the strictest confidence, by the lawyer and the lawyer's staff who may know information about your case. This assurance is referred to as client-lawyer privilege. Your lawyer is not allowed to discuss your case with anyone unless you are asked and you give express permission. The only circumstances in which a lawyer must reveal client information is if, by doing so, it prevents a crime or if your lawyer suspects you are committing child abuse. Lawyers and many other professionals are then required to notify police and the Children's Aid Society.

LEGAL AID

All provinces and territories have a fund available for people who cannot afford to pay a lawyer. To qualify for this assistance, you have to pass a means test to ensure you need the help. Then you get a certificate that you can present to a lawyer. Not all lawyers will do legal aid work, but those who do get paid a certain amount for each stage of the divorce process. This amount is usually lower than what you would normally pay for a lawyer yourself. The advantage to legal aid lawyers is that the amount they are paid is guaranteed. The advantage to you is that you will have adequate counsel.

To find legal aid services, look up legal aid in your phone book or check out their Web pages through **www.lawnet.com** or **www.canlaw.com**.

LAWYERS' FEES AND CONTRACTS

Lawyers' fees vary from province to province and from urban to rural areas. In general, junior lawyers who have only been practicing for a few years will charge between $80 to $120 an hour. Their more senior colleagues can charge anywhere from $175 and up. Most lawyers keep track of the time they spend on a case by dividing the hour into tenths or ten parts of six minutes each. If you spend two minutes on the phone with your lawyer, you will be charged for six minutes of his or her time (the smallest division) – from $8 to $25. Throughout a given hour a lawyer may work on several different cases so this is the way they keep track of their time. This information is calculated at regular intervals so the lawyer knows how much time is being spent on each case. Ordinarily, you will be billed for services on a monthly or quarterly basis.

In most cases a lawyer will insist on a retainer. You should too. A retainer can be both a written contract between you and the lawyer, as well as a lump sum of money paid as an advance. The retainer will outline the terms of the work to be done and the hourly rate, as well as the amount of the advance. A financial retainer can vary from a few hundred to thousands of dollars, depending on the complexity of the case. Make sure you get the retainer in writing. It could come in handy later if you have a dispute over your lawyer's bill.

You could include clauses in the contract that you wish the retainer to be renegotiated after specific stages in the divorce process. This will give you control of the amount of time and money the lawyer will be able to bill before re-examining the progress of the case. As written retainers are general practice for lawyers, do not consider hiring a lawyer who will not give you one.

Make sure you understand the terms of the retainer and make sure that it reflects your needs and desires. This first or second meeting is the time to establish your relationship with your lawyer on a sound footing. Be as clear as possible in the beginning about your expectations and what you can afford. A good lawyer will respect your interests and be willing to discuss openly aspects of the fee payment that you may be unfamiliar with.

Lawyers in Canada are not yet allowed to work on a contingency basis whereby the client agrees in advance to give the lawyer a percentage of the final settlement. They want to be paid up front. Many people prefer to pay their lawyers at regular intervals to avoid a large bill at the end of the case. In this way you can keep track of your expenditures and question any problems you have along the way. This can be an important reality check if your case is dragging on.

What could it cost? It's virtually impossible to estimate the final cost of a divorce because each case is different. Nonetheless, here's a rough guide based on a fee of $125 per hour:

Simple separation and divorce	No children, no pensions, no serious arguments about the breakup or property	$800 to $1,500 for each party
Simple divorce	Family with children, but the divorce is amicable	$1,000 to $3,000 for each party
Usual divorce	Some disagreements over property or handling of children, but both parties amicable	$2,000 to $5,000 for each party
More complex divorce	Disagreements over property, pension division, children; resolved by negotiation	$4,000 to $10,000 for each party
Difficult divorce	Anger from one partner; disagreement on all aspects; finally leading to time spent arguing before a judge	$12,000 to $30,000 for each party
Protracted divorce	Years of arguing, court appearances, legal wrangles with significant property at stake	Sky's the limit

Additional expenses On top of the lawyer's hourly rate, you will also be charged for other incidental costs. These include charges for producing and submitting various documents to the courts, photo-copying, couriers, etc. If your spouse's whereabouts are unknown, it will cost still more to track the person down and serve the spouse with the appropriate papers. Make sure you are aware of what these costs will be beforehand as you may prefer to take action yourself rather than have it done by an attorney.

Having problems with your lawyer's bill? Depending on the length of your case and the amount of work involved, the final bill often comes as quite a shock. This can be true even if you are reasonably satisfied with the outcome. If you are not (and this is often the case), it feels like rubbing salt into the wounds. If you feel that you are being overcharged, the first thing you should do is check over your retainer and any bill accounting you have received and then go and talk to your lawyer well prepared. If you make a good case, your lawyer may reconsider your bill and give you a discount. If you still feel your lawyer is charging too much, you can have the bill "taxed" or "accessed." This is an accepted practice in most provinces and requires you to take your complaint to a special tribunal of lawyers who will evaluate the bill. Check with your provincial law society to find out how to do this.

Changing your lawyer At some point throughout the legal process you may decide that you would rather be represented by someone else. You may be dissatisfied with the quality of work, with the communication between you or with any number of other issues. If you begin to feel you are not getting the type of service you were expecting, the first thing you need to do is meet with your lawyer to discuss your concerns. If you feel that things are not going to change, then let the lawyer know you are still dissatisfied and find someone else. The divorce process is difficult enough without being unhappy with your lawyer as well, but it will cause delays to change lawyers in mid-divorce.

Who pays court costs? You do, for the most part. Before 1968 and the new *Canadian Divorce Act*, court costs were usually paid by the husband, no matter what the outcome of the legal proceedings. Since then, there has been a dramatic change. It is now quite uncommon for a judge in a divorce proceeding to award costs to either spouse. The general practice is that the spouses pay their own legal costs.

In exceptional cases, though, where one spouse has been particularly difficult or has delayed the court proceedings irresponsibly, the judge may award costs to the winning party. Or if one spouse rejects a reasonable settlement before a trial begins and the final settlement turns out to be equal to or less than the proposed settlement, the judge may award costs to the successful spouse. In some cases, the ability of each party to pay is factored into the judge's decision. Whatever the situation, however, court-awarded costs will not cover all the legal bills of the successful spouse.

OTHER PROFESSIONALS

Although your lawyer will be the most important professional on your team, remember that he or she is there to take care of the legal aspects of your divorce. A lawyer is not also an accountant, counsellor or therapist. If you do try to use your lawyer for these purposes it can be a waste of money as most lawyers are not trained in these professions.

You'll need an accountant or actuary if there are considerable assets and liabilities to divide as a result of the divorce. It may be worthwhile to have an accountant review a draft financial settlement to ensure that the intent of the settlement will be met over the long term. This is especially true for tax purposes. If the value of a pension needs to be determined, you'll need an actuary. If you have given up a career to take care of the family, you might consider a vocational consultant who can give you an estimate on the earnings you may have forgone in order to take care of the family. You may also need a therapist for yourself or your children, or a mediator to discuss issues outside the courtroom.

Select these professionals in the same way your would choose your lawyer. If you do not know someone you trust, get recommendations from professional organizations or friends and check out a few before making a decision. And, of course, you are responsible for paying these professionals too.

THE DO-IT-YOURSELF DIVORCE

While it is almost always necessary to hire a lawyer to deal with a divorce or separation, it is sometimes possible to take care of the process yourself. The most favorable conditions for a do-it-yourself divorce are if you and your spouse agree on the breakup and there are no outstanding issues regarding property, support payments or parenting arrangements. The most appropriate circumstances are if your marriage was of a short duration with no children and no significant shared property or support issues to deal with. If this is your situation and one or both of you decide to take on the necessary paper and legal work, you must be prepared to spend the time to do it properly.

There are a number of excellent guides that will take you through the process, some of which can be found in the bibliography at the back of this book. The Web sites of the justice departments of federal and provincial governments offer excellent information on divorce and separation procedures.

It is always a good idea to have an experienced family lawyer review the relevant documents. You may have taken care of the most obvious issues like how to deal with the family home and the car but what about pensions, what about taxes? An agreement reached where either party is without legal counsel can easily be overturned in the courts later on.

Chapter Three

The separation and divorce process

A marriage breakup can be handled amicably and swiftly, sometimes in three or four months for the various stages from separation agreement to divorce. More commonly, there is a fairly quick separation agreement followed by a more protracted set of negotiations over the terms of the divorce. This often goes on for two years, sometimes even longer. If you or your former partner are angry, or refuse to negotiate fairly, the process of a divorce will drag on for years. Cases of eight, 10 and 12 years' duration are known to the courts. Obviously this is a considerable waste of time, money and emotional reserves.

Let's look at the various steps and stages from your initial decision to separate to the final divorce.

The process described here may vary slightly from jurisdiction to jurisdiction and from federal to provincial courts, but essentially it remains the same. Before beginning, here is a brief summary of the two general categories that divorce and separation fall into.

 One of the most important statistics to bear in mind when considering divorce is that 85 percent of divorces are uncontested. This means that the important issues of child custody and access, spousal and child support and division of property are worked out between the partners themselves, or with the help of a lawyer, without going through the court system.

THE UNCONTESTED DIVORCE

An uncontested divorce that is simple, meaning there are no important issues or there is agreement about them, will usually cost between $500 to $800. This type of divorce is straightforward and should not take a lawyer more than a few hours to deal with and will never require court time beyond a judge's signature on the final documents.

Even if there are major differences between a couple, there are many reasons why most disagreements about divorce and separation are settled out of court. One reason is that the Canadian court systems are overloaded and backlogged, so going to trial prolongs the divorce proceedings considerably. As a result, the longer a divorce takes, the more expensive it gets. Furthermore, there is no guarantee that either party to a divorce will get what they want out of a trial.

The added advantage of negotiation to a settlement is that the terms of the agreement are more likely to be adhered to by both parties if they agree to the terms. A settlement reached this way shows that both your and your ex are taking control of your own circumstances and are more likely to honor the agreements you reached than if you have to accept a court-imposed solution that you might strongly disagree with. In most cases it saves considerable time, frustration and money to settle rather than go to trial.

CONTESTED DIVORCE

A contested divorce is not about trying to prevent one spouse from getting a divorce by the other. In Canada, if one partner really wants out of a marriage there is little or nothing the other partner can do to stop it. A contested divorce, therefore, refers to disagreements between the spouses over spousal and child support, custody and access to the children, or division of property that are settled by going through the courts. Of the 15 percent of divorces that are contested, only 5 percent actually go to trial. Most contested divorces get resolved with a settlement negotiated between the spouses' respective lawyers – sometimes just hours before court begins. The final settlement is then presented to a judge for approval and authorization.

What is the cost of a contested divorce? There is no ceiling on a contested divorce. If spouses are prepared to fight each other to the bitter end, the cost of the divorce only depends on how much money the partners are willing to spend. Disputes over children, support and property can go on for a long time. The only sure thing about a contested divorce is that it will be stressful, slow and more expensive than you imagined. Everything else is unpredictable. Your very good lawyer may have a bad day in court when your case goes to trial. The judge may be cranky or overworked or have a personal agenda. If you are unhappy with the court settlement, it is possible to appeal, but this requires more time, stress and money, and there is no guarantee that the final judgment will be any different from the original.

Both the federal *Divorce Act* and provincial family laws apply to divorce settlements. Federal law governs the granting of divorce for a legally married couple. But the courts are also concerned about the welfare of children. Both provincial and federal laws have been harmonized so that when you apply to the federal court for a divorce, conditions affecting the children are also included. The only area that is exclusively a provincial jurisdiction are laws regarding the division of property. Again, with the aid of your lawyer, you can work out division of property, such as houses, real estate, cars, etc., in a negotiated settlement with your spouse and have these arrangements included in the federal petition for divorce.

If a couple wants to work out a separation agreement but not get a divorce, then issues such as custody, child and spousal support and property division are worked out through provincial family laws alone. This is also true for common-law couples who are separating as well. (See Chapter 9 for more information on common-law relationships.)

THE LEGAL PROCESS

What follows is a general overview of the legal process you go through when you apply to the courts for a divorce or separation. There are generally accepted rules, called the Rules of the Court, that have been developed to organize the process of various legal proceedings, divorce included. A divorce or separation can go through the following stages:

- exchange of lawyers' letters
- exchange of legal documents
- discovery or questioning of each other's case
- motions
- pretrials (discussions to try and find solutions to problems before they go to trial)
- trial
- appeal

A good rule to stay on top of your case, especially its cost, is to insist on getting a written evaluation from your lawyer on the probable outcome and cost of each stage in the process. This will force you to be very thoughtful about how to proceed and will keep you in control, or at least aware, of the costs as the process develops.

Exchange of letters If you have hired a lawyer to do your divorce, the lawyer will usually begin by sending a letter to your spouse or your spouse's lawyer, notifying them that you wish to work out a settlement regarding the marriage difficulties. This letter is very important as it can set the tone for all subsequent negotiations. The letter will also outline areas of concern or even suggest arrangements about child support, property division and other matters.

If you are seriously interested in searching for an equitable solution to the separation or divorce proceedings, make sure that you read the letter before it is sent and try and ensure that it is as personable as possible. You know your partner much better than your lawyer and you may be able to set the right tone for the correspondence. Lawyers' letters can go back and forth for months until a settlement is reached on all outstanding issues. If no settlement is possible, at least the major areas of difference between the parties will have been identified.

Exchange of legal documents If a settlement cannot be reached by an exchange of letters, then you can move to the next level – the civil law system. In effect you are saying, since it was not possible to work out our differences, we both want the court to make the decisions for us.

Divorce court proceedings can be started by submitting a standardized form, often called a divorce petition or application for divorce. This document contains the same information about who is involved in the dispute, the number of children, unresolved support and property issues, etc. The objective is to provide the court with as exact and detailed a description of the circumstances and positions involved in the dispute. Information to the court from each spouse is often provided as an affidavit, a document that has been legally witnessed stating that the information in the document is true. Financial statements outlining the financial resources and commitments are often included as well.

Copies of the documents are sent to your partner or partner's lawyer. If the whereabouts of your partner are unknown, a court can grant a substitute service, such as a notice in a newspaper, which will fulfill the legal requirement to serve the divorce petition. In some cases the court can even waive this requirement completely. If the documents are delivered to your spouse, make sure they are served in a discreet manner. If you have them delivered in such a way that your partner is embarrassed, this will only inflame an already charged situation.

The spouse who starts the divorce process is called the **petitioner** and the other, the **respondent**. If the respondent wishes to contest the divorce, he or she can file an answer, or an answer and a counter-petition. It is possible for a couple to file a joint petition for divorce based on the one-year separation criteria, although this option is still uncommon.

Once the documents have been served on the respondent, that person or his or her lawyer must prepare and deliver in writing a response called an **answer to the petition**, or if they wish, they can produce their own **counter-petition**. This will put forward their position regarding the proceedings along with appropriate affidavit and financial statements. In certain cases, you may have to prepare a reply to their material. All these documents, and they can become quite a few, are referred to as **the pleadings**. The pleadings outline all the issues in the case and, as clearly as possible, identify the outstanding differences.

Motions for interim orders Motions are requests to the court made by either side for decisions, or **temporary** or **interim orders** as they are called, by a judge on some issue related to the divorce or settlement. If granted, the motion stays in effect while the legal process is going on and can be either changed or removed as a result of a final trial or a settlement. Motions can be presented to the court at any time during the proceedings from the moment a divorce petition is submitted right up to the trial. They usually have to do with issues of child support, access or a request to stay in the family home, or they can deal with procedural matters to do with the case. (For more on court orders, see Chapter 10.)

If you are the spouse requesting a particular motion, you do not have to be present in court unless you want to be. What is necessary for the motion to be considered by the court is the motion itself and an affidavit from you outlining the reasons for the request. In certain situations of dire need, a court can make an "interim interim" order to take care of bare necessities like food and accommodation and even custody. In an emergency, these motions can be brought before a judge without notice to the other party.

A judge can make a decision that can be challenged by an opposing lawyer and will need to be heard before the judge at a later date to determine whether the interim interim order needs to be maintained or changed. If the other side wishes to, they can request an adjournment to go through the discovery process (see below) again regarding the requested motion. This will require recording and distribution of the questions and answers related to the motion. The matter is brought back to a judge for a decision and he or she may grant or deny the request – or come up with something in between. For instance, if a couple has separated, a wife may request an order for a specific amount of money for child support during the trial process. The husband may suggest something else and the final decision by a judge may be another figure altogether. The judge's decision becomes the legal decision of the court.

Again be aware that motions can be expensive, up to $2,000 plus expenses, and they are time consuming. Always try to work out these issues before they go to court.

Discovery   Discovery is the process by which each party in a divorce gets information on the other. For instance, you may think you know your partner's salary and how much money he or she has in the bank, but a divorce judgment will need exact figures. As well, many employees have pensions that must be evaluated and then divided between the two of you. Your house, if you own one, also has a value that must be determined. Getting exact data and evaluations is called the process of discovery. It takes time and money.

There are two parts to the discovery process: **documentary** and **oral**. Documentary discovery goes on between your lawyers. They need to be assured that all documents, including any computer disks, photographs, even drawings that will be used in a possible trial, will be available to the other side during the oral discovery. Both sides need to know what documents each will be presenting since you will not be permitted to produce a surprise document during a trial. (The reason for this is to avoid wasting the court's time with issues that could be solved before a trial.)

The oral discovery usually takes place in a room in the family law courts. It is the opportunity for the lawyer for your spouse to ask you questions about all the documents you have submitted in presenting your case. Your lawyer will be present to advise you if need be, as well as a reporter who records all the questions and answers during the discovery process. This process is repeated for your spouse by your lawyer at another time. The purpose of the discovery is for both lawyers to better understand the position of the other side, clarify issues and probe for weak areas in the other side's position.

These oral discoveries are written up by the court reporter and these transcripts are exchanged between the two sides. Any outstanding issues can be clarified at this point and the other side must provide the requested information. Again, at this stage both sides have made their respective positions clear and are now ready to go to trial.

Negotiation beats fighting

If you cannot settle your disputes by your-selves, the court will do it for you. This requires relinquishing control of the process and handing over to a judge the most important issues affecting your life, your children, support and property. There are some circumstances where this is unavoidable due to the anger and intransigence of one side or the other, but court action is never the best way to proceed.

The court process is slow and can be filled with post-ponements. To have all your personal and financial details open to public scrutiny at a trial that decides on issues affecting your economic well-being and the lives of your children is traumatic, to say the least. At the conclusion, it is rare that either side is happy with the court decisions.

For whatever reason you have ended up going to court, you need to prepare yourself as much as possible for what lies ahead. Do some more research into how the court works in the jurisdiction where you are applying. Get your lawyer to set up a tour of the court either by staff of the lawyer, or a court official if possible. This will familiarize you with the physical layout of the court and what goes on in its various rooms.

Aside from the emotional and psychological stress of a trial, a more up-front consideration is the cost involved in going through a complete trial. Once you have made a deci-sion (or the decision has been made for you) to go to trial, you need to sit down with your lawyer and get a realistic sense of what the process involves and the likely outcome. You need to re-examine your retainer with your lawyer and most likely he will insist on a cash advance before proceed-ing to trial. It is not unusual for a lawyer to request a retainer of $10,000 to $20,000, depending on the circum-stances of the case.

Court costs, including your lawyer's fees, can range

anywhere from $1,500 to $4,000 per day depending on the length of the trial. If you lose and you were presented with an **offer to settle** that approximates the final judgment before the trial began, you will be required to pay a portion of the winner's legal costs. Again, only the wealthy or people who qualify for legal aid can easily afford to go to trial. Others who go this route will often go into serious debt, one that offsets or eliminates whatever award the court finally makes.

PRETRIAL

Often referred to as a settlement conference, a pretrial meeting between the principals involved in a divorce case is designed to work out the major difference in the case *before* the case goes in front of a judge. A pretrial is a formal procedure presided over by a judge who will not be the one to hear the case if it goes to trial; sometimes this is done before another experienced court official. Except in unusual circumstance, both you and your spouse should be present at these pretrial proceedings.

To begin, the pretrial judge or court official will examine all the pleadings and ask you both any questions he or she may need to understand the case better. Again the purpose of the pretrial is to attempt to resolve some or all of the differences between you. An experienced court official can often accomplish a lot during these five-way discussions and can have a great influence on both you and your lawyers if the court official gives opinions about how issues are likely to be resolved during a trial.

If the pretrial stage is unsuccessful in resolving any disagreements, then those that remain unresolved go to trial.

THE TRIAL

The way trial dates are set varies from jurisdiction to jurisdiction. Some provincial courts have what is known as a fixed system where lawyers inform the court that they are prepared for trial and are assigned a specific date the trial will begin. Other provinces "overbook" the courts by selecting a number of cases to be ready to go to trial during a specific week. This method is partially based on the assumption that some parties will settle their disputes before going to trial. This method avoids the possibility of wasting the court's time preparing for a trial that never takes place.

Even though you have a fixed date, circumstances can develop that force a postponement of your trial. These delays can be very disruptive to everyone especially the spouses and any witnesses that might be called to testify to prove the case. They may show up, wait for hours and sometimes days, and then be sent home to wait for another trial date.

The normal process of a trial follows five steps:

1. introduction and opening statements
2. the petitioner's (or plaintiff's) case
3. the respondent's (or defendant's) case
4. summation
5. judgment

Introduction and opening statements After the judge enters the courtroom and the trial gets underway, the lawyer for the petitioner, who brought to case to court, and the lawyer for the respondent briefly summarize their case for the judge. They may also deal with administrative details of the case and mention which witnesses will be called on behalf of each side.

The petitioner's case Once these preliminaries are out of the way, the judge will instruct the lawyer for the petitioner to call the first witness. This is usually the petitioner, who tells his or her story. Then other witnesses may be called to support the petitioner's story. A witness may not be allowed in the courtroom while the trial is going on and cannot even talk to other witnesses to avoid the possibility of influencing each other about what they will say during the trial.

A good lawyer will review beforehand with the petitioner and witnesses how best to give evidence. Usually the lawyer for the petitioner will ask open-ended questions. This means not asking questions that suggest the answer the lawyer is looking for. Generally lawyers advise witnesses to give evidence in a clear, confident voice and to direct their remarks at the judge. When you are questioned, only answer the question being asked and do not speculate about the answer if you don't know it.

After the petitioner's lawyer has asked witnesses about all the information his or her client wants to put before the court, then the lawyer for the respondent will have the opportunity to ask more questions, or to cross-examine, the petitioner's witnesses.

In this case the lawyer for the respondent will ask leading questions that only require a yes or no answer. A general lawyers' rule is never ask a question to which your side does not know the answer already. The object of this exercise is to try and point out contradictions or inconsistencies in a witness's testimony. This weakens the witness's evidence and the argument the petitioner's lawyer is developing. After these questions are answered, if there are any, the judge can ask questions for further clarification of what has been said. This process if followed for each witness.

The respondent's case The process described above is repeated with the respondent and any witnesses the respondent's lawyer may call to give evidence. The petitioner's lawyer is also allowed to call a witness if the respondent's witnesses introduce new information that the petitioner's lawyer needs to deal with.

Testimony rarely goes as smoothly as this summary suggests. What happens in reality is that there are usually numerous disruptions to the flow of the trial made by people coming and going from the courtroom, adjournments because witnesses did not appear, the availability of the judge or other interruptions.

Summation After the principals and witnesses have been examined and re-examined and the judge has had to opportunity to ask any questions, both lawyers sum up their case. They draw on the evidence presented to the court throughout the trial, then weave into the summation relevant points of law and previous cases to strengthen their arguments. As the summation proceeds, each lawyer will make recommendations about how various outstanding disputes should be resolved.

When this process has finished the judge may ask further clarifying questions about each lawyer's case. Then the trial is adjourned. Throughout the trial, the judge has been making notes on key points. Now the judge gathers together these notes and other proceedings of the trial in order to make a decision.

It is very rare for a judge to make a decision immediately when the trial is over. What usually happens is the judge will "reserve judgment" until a later date when a written judgment will be handed down. The trial is adjourned and everyone goes on with their lives while they wait for the judge to make a decision. This part of the process can take several months or longer.

The judgment At some point the lawyers are informed that the judge has made a decision and produced what is known as the **reasons for the judgment**. This outlines what reasons the judge used to made various decisions regarding the case. The lawyers have an opportunity to ask the judge for clarification if they are not clear on certain aspects of the reasoning. Then the actual decisions on the outstanding issues are put into a separate judgment. Once the lawyers accept these decisions, the judgment is recorded and becomes effective.

At this point the lawyers meet with the judge to determine who will pay the court costs. If a previous offer to settle is introduced at this point by either party that is close to the decision made by the judge, then considerable court costs can be assessed to that person.

Appeals It is possible to appeal the decision of the judge in these cases. It is not uncommon for either or both lawyers to identify what they consider to be errors in law made by the judge. In other words, a lawyer may believe the judge made a mistake in applying a principle of law or interpreting a piece of legislation. If the appeal is based on a sound argument, then the issue can be taken to a higher level of the legal system. If the appeal is successful, the loser can then re-appeal until the case reaches the Supreme Court of Canada.

Before deciding to appeal to a higher court level, you should have a serious consultation with your lawyer. The appeal process will cost as much or more than the original court proceedings and will be just as long. The outcome will be just as uncertain. And the same cost rules apply – the loser of the appeal is liable for the legal costs of the winner. A very serious issue must be at stake before you contemplate an appeal. Others who come after you may benefit from your successful appeals, but you might well be the loser.

Case study: John and Caitlin

John and Caitlin had been married for five years when Caitlin announced that she no longer loved her husband and wanted to move in with Henry, her supervisor at work. John was hurt and angry, certainly not amenable to an easy divorce. Complicating the entire situation was Shauna, their two-year-old daughter.

After getting some preliminary legal advice, Caitlin got a furnished apartment and moved with Shauna into their new, temporary home. (She wisely decided not to move in with Henry at this point.) She had her lawyer send a letter to John asking for temporary support of $1,200 a month and offered once-a-month visitation.

John immediately hired a lawyer who responded that $1,200 a month was far too much money given their incomes and that John wanted joint custody of the child. Letters and counter-letters went back and forth over a period. John and Caitlin tried to talk through the issues, but John's anger was so intense and Caitlin was so defensive that they could make little progress themselves. At this point, both sides legal bills had reached about $3,000. After three months, Caitlin's lawyer said they would have to go before a judge with a motion to seek an interim judgment to set some sort of terms for both parties.

A judge looked at the pleadings for an interim judgment. She awarded Caitlin temporary child support of $450 a month denied John's pleading for joint custody, and giving John access to Shauna every weekend, from Friday night to Sunday noon.

This preliminary judgment had raised their legal fees beyond the $4,000 mark.

At this point, John and Caitlin were legally separated, but certainly not divorced. Caitlin was not really free to pursue her relationship with Henry (and certainly not free to remarry), nor could John really begin moving on to a new life as a single dad with obligations to his young daughter. Both parties needed a divorce, but were far apart on the final terms.

Time is sometimes a wonderful balm for legal squabbles. In this case, a year of legal discovery and personal cooling down made both parties more reasonable about settlement. John gave up his quest for joint custody, which would never have been granted because Caitlin opposed it so adamantly, and he no longer wanted to end the marriage on the grounds of adultery. Caitlin decided to settle for the usual federal child-support guidelines (about $400 a month) and withdraw her claim for spousal support since she made more money than John did. The only outstanding issue was child access, which the two finally resolved with a compromise.

The final agreement did not require presenting before a judge. It was agreed on by John and Caitlin, then sent for judicial approval by their lawyers. The final bill: $5,500 to each lawyer for time spent; $1,200 in associated expenses for copying and related court fees; and $1,500 to actuaries for evaluating pensions.

Chapter Four

The legal divorce

The *Divorce Act* is federal legislation that provides federal courts with the authority to legally terminate marriages and to issue orders on child custody, parental access, child and spousal support payments and other matters. Although responsibilities such as child and spousal support, custody and access arrangements can exist and often change after the divorce, once the divorce process has been finalized by the legal system, the marriage itself is over.

Over the past 40 years there have been substantial changes to the laws governing divorce in Canada. In 1968 and 1985, there were significant legal changes that made it much easier to get a divorce than in the past. It was the *Divorce Act* of 1985 that introduced into law the concept of no-fault divorce.

The 1985 *Divorce Act* declared that "marriage breakdown" is the only grounds for divorce in Canada. The Act defined this in three ways:

1. The spouses have lived separately and apart for at least a year.
2. Either spouse has committed adultery.
3. Either spouse has subjected the other to intolerable physical or mental cruelty.

Let's examine each more carefully.

SEPARATION

A one-year separation period for a no-fault divorce is the way more than 80 percent of couples get divorced in Canada. The advantage of this approach to marriage breakdown is that there is no need to lay blame or describe the difficulties of the marriage. The proof of marriage breakdown is the separation itself.

There are a few wrinkles, of course. In order for the separation to be accepted in court, it must be a result of difficulties in the marriage. For instance, a husband or wife cannot file for divorce if it was mutually agreed that the other goes to work in New Zealand for a year. The one-year separation must also be continuous. For instance if a couple separates for six months, then gets back together for four months, but then separates again, neither party can claim the initial six month as part of the one-year separation. They have to be separated for a year from the second time they separated. There is an exception to every rule and because the courts would rather see couples reconcile, the law does allow for couples to get back together for a period of 90 days. If the period of reconciliation is more than 90 days, they have to start the one-year period over again.

Unless there are serious reasons like domestic abuse, most lawyers will recommend that the no-fault procedure be followed. Using the argument of adultery or cruelty can put an accused spouse on the defensive and can create difficulties with court orders regarding custody, support or property division.

Usually, living separately and apart means living in separate residences. Usually one of the spouses will move out of the family home and live somewhere else. In some circumstances, often for financial reasons, it is not possible for a couple to live separately. A couple can still claim to be separated while living together in the family home as long as they do not have sexual relations, they sleep and eat separately, and to the greatest extent possible lead separate lives. As the courts do not take separation lightly, the onus is on the couple to prove that they are living separate lives even though they are together under the same roof. This is a very difficult circumstance to maintain for a year, so most couples made alternate living arrangements.

Either spouse can file for divorce as soon as the separation takes place, but the courts will not grant a divorce until a full year has passed since the date of separation. If adultery or cruelty has occurred during the separation period, the non-offending spouse can petition for divorce immediately or can wait for the no-fault separation period to run out. If the divorce petition is made after the one-year separation period has passed, the divorce judgment can be made right away.

> Although it requires a wait, separation is the simplest, least contentious way to get a divorce.

ADULTERY

As marriage breakdown is the only reason for granting a divorce, adultery is not truly a grounds for divorce. However, if adultery can be proved, then marriage breakdown can be established immediately. A judge can then grant a divorce as soon as the case can be brought to court.

Adultery occurs when a married person has voluntary sexual intercourse with someone of the opposite sex who is not their spouse. Heavy petting, mutual masturbation, oral sex or other forms of sexual activity does not qualify as adultery. Neither does homosexual or lesbian sex. Unless adultery is admitted, it must be proven in court.

Again there are wrinkles. No matter how difficult a marriage might be, a spouse cannot get out of it by committing adultery. Only the non-offending spouse can apply for a divorce as a result of adultery. If both partners in a marriage have committed adultery, it is possible for both parties to apply for a divorce citing the adultery of the other spouse.

The charge of adultery is used less and less in the divorce proceedings. People are rarely caught in the act of adultery these days. Proving adultery can take up considerable time and expense through hiring private detectives or finding witnesses. However, circumstantial evidence such as love letters, incriminating hotel receipts, the transmission of sexual diseases, can all be used as proof of adultery. Although it is difficult to prove, a judge will look for "evidence of association, inclination and opportunity."

Overall, lawyers are reluctant to file for divorce on the grounds of either adultery or mental cruelty. It is much simpler and less expensive to wait for the one-year separation for no-fault divorce. It is believed that if a spouse wishes a divorce based on the offense of adultery or cruelty, then there are usually ulterior motives or other circumstances that drive this approach. These may have to do with property division or child access or custody.

 It is also adultery if a married person who is separated has sex with a member of the opposite sex. According to the law the marriage is still in effect even though the spouses are living separate lives.

CRUELTY

The third circumstance under which a spouse can prove marriage breakdown is physical or mental cruelty. The cruelty must be so severe as to make it intolerable for one of the spouses to remain living with the other. Cruelty is defined the way everyone understands the word: "a disposition to inflict pain and suffering, delight in or indifference to the pain or suffering of others, or mercilessness or hard-heartedness." It must involve serious and grave behavior that a spouse should not be expected to put up with. Cruelty does not include unhappiness or incompatibility or the normal disagreements that may occur between couples in a marriage.

There are still grey areas. Judges tend to believe that cruelty it often a matter of fact and degree. Often it depends on the personalities of the couple, the history of their marital relations and their attitudes toward the marriage. A judge will take these factors into consideration before making a ruling on a divorce petition based on the grounds of cruelty.

In difficult cases, the legal test of cruelty can be quite subjective. What a judge has to decide is whether the behavior of one spouse in a marriage is serious enough to prevent the other spouse from staying in the relationship. In most cases, it is not necessary to provide proof of bodily or mental harm, nor is the intention of the spouse who carries out the cruelty relevant to the court's deliberations. All that matters is the effect of the behavior on the victim.

Behavior that has been considered cruelty in Canadian case law includes:

- excessive sexual demands
- persistent refusal to have marital sex
- sexual deviancy or unorthodoxy
- alcoholism or drug addiction
- threatening insults
- persistent refusal to communicate with the other spouse

Physical cruelty includes everything from punching and slapping to threatening, throwing, locking in rooms, etc.

To repeat: A spouse cannot commit cruelty and then apply to the courts for a speedy divorce. Only the spouse who believes he or she was abused can apply for divorce and they should do it at the time the cruelty becomes intolerable.

 Cases of physical abuse are most often obvious and need to be acted on immediately. Physical or sexual abuse within a relationship clearly constitutes cruelty and courts will generally act quickly to provide divorce in these circumstances.

PREVENTING DIVORCE

In certain circumstances a spouse can prevent a divorce from being granted. These circumstances are often referred to as the four C's. Except for child support, these bars to divorce rarely appear in court cases:

1. collusion
2. connivance
3. condonation
4. child support

Collusion refers to a deliberate attempt on the part of both spouses to deceive the court by intentionally suppressing evidence that is relevant to their divorce petition. If the court discovers that there has been collusion between the spouses, the judge must dismiss the divorce petition.

Connivance is considered a provisional bar to divorce that can prevent the divorce from occurring or let it proceed depending on the circumstances. Connivance usually occurs in relation to adultery. It refers to any conduct that either spouse carries out that encourages the other spouse to commit an offense. So if a couple voluntarily takes part in group sex with other partners, neither one can then turn around and petition the court for a divorce since they were both aware and presumably encouraged the adultery. A partner who knowingly allows adultery to happen is guilty of connivance.

Condonation only applies in divorce petitions that are based on adultery or cruelty. It refers to one of the spouses forgiving the other for the cruelty or adultery that occurred. Unlike connivance and collusion, condonation is considered praiseworthy. The courts always encourage couples to reconcile. If a couple continues living together after an adultery has been discovered, the courts will consider that the offense has been forgiven.

Although condonation applies to cruelty as well, the courts generally do not consider it in effect if the wife stays in an abusive relationship. In such a situation it may be because she hopes her partner will stop the abuse, she may not have the funds to relocate or she may stay in a relationship for the sake of the children. Just because a spouse may stay in an abusive relationship does not mean that the courts will consider the spouse to be condoning the abuse.

Condonation is a provisional bar to divorce. Even when it is proved in court, the judge may still grant a divorce if he or she believes it is in the public interest. There is a general belief that a spouse should not be penalized if that spouse eventually decides to request a divorce after putting up with abuse for some time.

Child support is a primary concern of the courts. Whether a divorce petition is submitted on the grounds of separation, adultery or cruelty, the courts must ensure that any children of the marriage are adequately provided for.

It is not enough for a divorce petition to state that adequate financial provisions have been made for the children. In a contested or uncontested divorce (see Chapter 4), the petition must outline in some detail the income and assets of each spouse and specified arrangements for regular payment. If these details are not included, the court will deny a divorce until they are produced.

The courts try not to discriminate between rich and poor people by denying divorce to people who cannot afford to adequately provide for their children after divorce. In cases where child support cannot be provided, social assistance is taken into consideration.

Other restrictions on divorce The 1985 *Divorce Act* governs the right of Canadians to get divorced according to the laws of the state. It does not regulate the rules that apply to religious divorces or annulments. For example, a Roman Catholic can get a state-sanctioned divorce through the Canadian federal courts but this does not qualify as a divorce within the Catholic Church. Although divorce is not allowed within the Catholic Church, annulments are. Annulments are administered through the Church under the Code of Canon Law. A Roman Catholic must get an annulment of the first marriage before he or she can get remarried within the Church. This does not apply to remarrying within state law as in a civil ceremony, only to church law.

Foreign divorce According to the *Divorce Act*, Canada recognizes divorces that take place in other countries as long as at least one of the spouses was normally a resident of that country prior to the divorce, or was resident in that country for a minimum of a year before divorce proceedings were undertaken.

It is also possible to get a divorce in Canada even if you were married in another country, as long as you meet Canadian residency requirements.

At this time, divorced spouses cannot apply to the Canadian courts for support from a spouse if their divorce took place in another country. Only people who normally reside in Canada can apply to the courts for support orders.

THE DIVORCE PROCEDURE

As the *Divorce Act* is federal legislation, it applies to all provinces and territories in Canada. It refers only to the dissolution of the marriage and not to other important matters like support payments, custody and access issues and the division of property. Later chapters will deal with these important issues in detail.

Only federally appointed judges can make decisions regarding divorce. The courts in which a divorce can be tried are called by different names depending on the province. In British Columbia, the federal court is called the Supreme Court of British Columbia. In Alberta, Saskatchewan, Manitoba and New Brunswick it is referred to as the Court of Queen's Bench, while in Ontario it is called the Ontario Superior Court of Justice. In other provinces and territories divorces can be handled within district or county courts. Some provinces are beginning to also use unified family courts. Whatever they are called, it is only these courts that can deal with divorce. A divorce granted in one jurisdiction is legal in all the other provinces and territories in the country.

Divorce petitions must be filed in the province or territory where the petitioner is normally resident. To be accepted, the spouse applying for divorce must have lived in the province where the petition is filed for at least one year before divorce proceedings were begun.

This regulation is in place in order to prevent spouses from shopping around for the least expensive or complicated divorce procedure. It also prevents one spouse from choosing a location that would be extremely inconvenient to the other spouse.

Residency is not the only criteria for choosing the location to begin divorce proceedings. The welfare of any children of the marriage is also taken into consideration. For instance, if a husband in Toronto applies for a divorce from his wife who is living with their children in Vancouver, the court reserves the right to transfer the case to British Columbia. It is considered in the best interest of the children to do this because then the people most involved with the children's lives would be available to have input into the case. Choice of location is also important because property division legalities vary from province to province.

If each spouse files for divorce separately in different provinces, the petition that has been filed first will decide which province the divorce will take place in. If by chance both spouses apply for divorce on the same day but in different provinces, then the divorce is heard in a special court called the Trial Division of the Federal Court.

The right to remarry A spouse has the right to legally remarry in a civil ceremony 31 days after the granting of the divorce decree. This one-month waiting period is there to allow time for an appeal by either party to the divorce. If a spouse gets married before the month has passed, he or she can be charged with bigamy, a federal offense in Canada. Exceptions can be made to this rule if there is a pressing need declared by one of the divorced partners. For instance, if the husband's girlfriend is pregnant and about to give birth, the court may waive the 31 day waiting period so that the child can be born within a new marriage.

 The information in this book is accurate up to the year 2001, but no book can cover all the legal issues involved in a divorce in the particular jurisdiction where you live. Always consult an attorney to get up to date and specific information regarding your personal circumstances.

Chapter Five

Other ways to settle your differences

There are many reasons for seeking out alternatives to the legal process to resolve conflicts that develop in divorce and separation. The court system encourages lawyers for each side to develop positions that they argue as best they can in front of a judge to see who will "win." For people already under a great deal of stress, choosing winners and losers is not the best way to solve complex family problems.

Solutions that are forced on a couple will often not be honored no matter what the legal consequences might be. As a result there is an increasing use of alternative methods for resolving marital disputes. Here are some to consider.

RECONCILIATION

The Canada *Divorce Act* requires all lawyers to inform people who approach them about divorce about available marriage reconciliation services. The general position taken by the courts is that separation and divorce are actions of last resort and every effort should be made to facilitate a marriage reconciliation. In rare cases, a judge might even stop a divorce trial if she believes a couple is interested in exploring ways to reconcile their differences and get back together. Unfortunately these statutory obligations for lawyers and courts to try and help couples to reconcile have not be very successful. More often than not, by the time a spouse approaches a lawyer concerning a divorce, one partner or the other considers the marriage to be over. If a lawyer believes there is little hope for reconciliation, he may do little more than inform you of the reconciliation resources available in your area and leave it at that. (Do your research and find out which marriage counsellors are in your area.)

NEGOTIATIONS

Most divorce and separation settlements are arrived at between lawyers through an exchange of letters or face-to-face meetings. These negotiations can go on for months or can be settled very quickly, depending on the complexity of the issues and the good will of the parties involved. This is the most common way to arrive at a divorce or separation agreement. This process need not involve a court order beyond final approval of the agreement.

MEDIATION

Mediation is another method that lawyers are obliged to inform their clients about. The mediation process involves a couple both agreeing to engage a third person to help them reach a consensus on outstanding issues related to their separation. In many ways this is preferable to court action, for many couples feel resentful or powerless when major decisions affecting their lives are taken over by the courts. Using mediation, a couple can feel much more in control of major decision that affect their lives and are also much more likely to keep to the terms of an agreement that they have worked out by themselves.

Choosing the right mediator is as important as choosing the right lawyer.

Although it is an increasingly important and demanded service, at the present time there are no specific criteria or professional standards for qualifying as a mediator. Many professionals, such as lawyers, doctors and social workers, have developed mediation skills and taken training. On the other hand, there are some mediators whose only qualifications seem to be that they went through a bad divorce themselves. They may have considerable empathy but very little objective experience.

Take the time to interview a number of mediators and make sure there is good chemistry between you before you decide. And remember that your partner has to agree as well. Your lawyer should be able to recommend experienced mediators or you may hear of someone through friends. The Department of justice in Ottawa has also compiled a list of mediators available across the country.

Mediation services vary from province to province. In some provinces, mediation is free and provided for by the courts. In others, it is different. For instance, in Montreal mediation services on all issues related to separation and divorce are free, while in Quebec City, free mediation only applies to issues concerning children. In Ontario, mediation costs are covered by legal aid certificates if you qualify for assistance; otherwise you pay an hourly rate. Your lawyer should be able to advise you on the services where you live.

Mediators are somewhat less expensive than lawyers and their cost is shared by both spouses. Fees can range from $50 to $150 an hour, depending on qualifications, experience and location.

Mediation usually follows the same process. There is an initial meeting where the mediator will meet with both spouses to sort out and clarify the main issues in dispute. Then suggested solutions will be explored and, from those, some possible solutions will be agreed on. Finally, whatever is agreed on will be written up for both sides to consider. The objective of mediation is always to have the parties in dispute come up with mutually agreed-on solutions. Experience has proven that this method of arriving at solutions is the most likely to last over time.

The mediator will usually ask you whether you want the discussions to be open or closed. If they are open, this means that anything said can by used in court if there is no ultimate mediation settlement. If they are closed, then the information discussed during mediation is confidential and cannot be used in legal proceedings. This is a decision you both need to make with your lawyers.

All issues in a divorce or separation are open to mediation, although some mediators may specialize in certain areas such as issues relating to children or division of property.

Lawyers are essential to this mediation process as well. Ideally the mediator and the lawyers will work closely together to ensure that any agreements worked out during the process will be acceptable in a court of law. Lawyers may also rewrite the mediator's recommendations so they comply with court criteria and procedures.

Remember that mediation is not marriage counselling or therapy. Its purpose is not to find out why you are having difficulties in your relationship. The primary focus of mediation is on settling differences about your breakup. In this sense, the process is about your future, not the past.

Mediators preform a variety of functions during the mediation process. They must

- be impartial, as both of you are clients
- act as moderator, but not make any decisions regarding the disputed issues
- maintain confidentiality
- develop an atmosphere of trust and good will
- compensate for differences in negotiating skills between spouses
- ensure that domestic violence or child abuse is not occurring

The mediator will also take care of administrative issues like co-ordinating meetings, keep both lawyers informed of progress, provide relevant information like child support criteria and write up the agreed-upon solutions to differences.

Although mediation is an increasingly popular method of resolving disputes between couples, it is not for everyone. It must be voluntarily undertaken and both parties have to agree to participate, otherwise it is impossible to mediate successfully.

There are also a number of circumstances where mediation is not suitable. It is not appropriate if there is a large power disparity between couples. If one spouse holds all the cards, it is very difficult for there to be an equitable, fair negotiation process, no matter how hard a mediator tries to bring balance to the process. It is also not appropriate if there is a history of domestic violence as the abused partner is not in a good position to negotiate. Finally, it is not appropriate if there is child abuse. If child abuse is discovered or strongly suspected during the mediation process, the mediator is obliged to report it to the authorities, who will intervene to protect the child.

In summary, the mediation process can be quick and relatively inexpensive relative to the costs of a trial. In many cases, you and your partner will be pleased with the results you have achieved and are more likely to adhere to the terms as a result. Finally, many people learn mediation and negotiating skills they can use with their former partner in the future and in other situations.

ARBITRATION

Arbitration is another method for resolving marital disputes that draws on the pattern of labor negotiating. As with labor-management conflicts, there is the perception that ex-spouses are going to have to go on working together, especially if there are children involved. This provides strong motivation to try and reconcile the parties as much as possible in order to preserve a workable relationship.

What happens in arbitration is that both parties select a mutually agreeable third party to hear both sides of the issues. This person then provides resolutions to the conflicts that you and your partner must agree to. This is called binding arbitration. Both sides have to agree to abide by the arbitrator's decision. The arbitrator is often an experienced professional in family law, sometimes a retired judge.

The main advantage of this option for resolving marital disputes is that the proceedings are private. All the details – custody, access, finances, support, property division – are confidential, unlike courts proceedings that are open to the public and the press. The arbitration method is also much faster than the public court system. Arbitration decisions are often rendered within 30 days. There may also be an advantage for the couple being able to choose who will make the decision in their case. Arbitrators are most often interested and experienced in family law and so are ideally placed to make good decisions. This is not always the case with publicly appointed trial judges, who can get randomly assigned to family law cases.

The downside of arbitration is that it can be expensive. Both you and your partner will not only have to pay the cost of your lawyers, but of the arbitrator as well. If a judge, this person can charge anywhere from $2,000 to $3,000 for hearing the case. The cost of an arbitrator is not covered by legal aid and has to be shared by both spouses.

However, for those who can afford it, the speed and privacy of this method can make it an attractive option. Again your lawyer should be able to advise you on a good arbitrator if you decide to go this route.

SETTLING YOUR DIFFERENCES

The best approach to separation and divorce, if all efforts at reconciliation have failed, is to arrive at a negotiated settlement as quickly and equitably as possible. Not withstanding the difficult emotional experience for everyone involved in separation, the quicker an equitable settlement is arrived at, the quicker the partners can get on with their lives.

The central issues in family breakups are child custody and access, child and spousal support, division of property and other related issues. Other areas a negotiated agreement can deal with include

- indexation of support payments with the cost of living
- restriction on the mobility of the custodial parent
- restrictions on changing children's names without the consent of the other spouse
- division of pensions
- health and medical expenses
- effects of getting back together

However, even if a couple develops a settlement by themselves, with lawyers or other professionals, without engaging with the legal system, they still have to make their settlement "within the shadow of the law." This means that whatever settlement they arrive at has to conform to the laws regarding divorce and separation before they can be formalized by the legal system.

Since the majority of relationship breakdowns are settled out of court, it is useful to get an overview of the process and the various documents that detail the settlement between the two parties.

(All provinces and territories have similar documents, although they may be called slightly different names.) The four main ones are

1. offers to settle
2. minutes of settlement
3. orders of consent
4. separation agreements

Offers to settle come in two forms – informal and formal. Informal offers can be letters or conversations exchanged between lawyers during the negotiation process. This process can be short or long, simple or complicated, depending on the circumstances of the separation or divorce. Experienced lawyers are aware that, depending on timing and circumstances, equitable settlements can be arrived at with astute negotiation skills. A wife may be prepared to give up claims on certain property or pension credits in exchange for sole possession of the family home. A husband may be prepared to pay a specified amount of child support if he is guaranteed certain access arrangements that he wants. Eventually the back and forth between the lawyers can end in an agreement that both spouses are satisfied with. In this case, an offer to settle will be made by one of the lawyers and sent to the other spouse. These kinds of offers can be sent with the disclaimer that they are being presented "without prejudice," meaning that the offer is for negotiation only and cannot be used at a later date in court.

Formal offers to settle would not contain this disclaimer and are meant as a serious offer of settlement. In this instance, if the offer is not accepted and the case goes to court and the final judgment is close to the formal offer to settle, then one spouse may be liable for a portion of all legal costs from the time the offer was made right up until the final judgment.

Formal offers to settle are registered with the court and become official documents in the case. Because the offers to settle produced by lawyers during the negotiation process can be open to interpretation, judges have begun to insist that the offers be written on standardized official court documents that make it clear what is being agreed to by both parties.

Formal offers to settle can put considerable pressure on both parties to make sure they are confident about the outcome of court proceedings before they are initiated.

If either the informal or court-produced formal offers to settle are accepted, then the case moves on to the next documents.

Minutes of settlement are basically a written summary of agreements that have been arrived at between the parties, concerning the various aspects of the separation or divorce. Once these minutes of settlement have been signed by both spouses and witnessed (usually by the lawyers involved), they become binding and enforceable. To make the settlement even more secure, the lawyers may get the agreement incorporated into another court document called an order on consent.

Orders of consent At this point either lawyer can present the minutes of settlement to a judge to have them incorporated into an order of consent that formalizes the agreement and further attests to the fact that all parties agree that the settlement is acceptable to everyone involved.

SEPARATION AGREEMENTS

Often referred to as a "legal" settlement, this document sets out the terms of separation between a couple who are legally married or living in a common-law relationship. As mentioned earlier, this is by far the most common method of settling family law disputes. Separation agreements can also be arrived at any time after court proceedings have begun if the couple realizes it is in their best interest to settle their disputes without going all the way through court proceedings.

There are a number of very good reasons to reach a separation agreement even under the most favorable circumstances. The process of arriving at a settlement can produce a healthy reality check. In the best of circumstances, it forces a couple to deal with issues that effect both them and their children. The process can also produce closure to the past relationship so that the former partners can get on with their lives. Another reason for producing a settlement agreement that is written down in black and white is that it becomes an important reference document as time goes by and memories change.

Legal separation agreements are also enforceable in every province and territory across the country and, in certain provinces, can be filed with support enforcement agencies as if they were court orders. This is most useful where a spouse needs to enforce support payments that have fallen into arrears.

A written agreement of some sort is also required for tax considerations. If there is an agreement, spousal support payments can be deducted from taxable income in the case of the payer and need to be declared as taxable income by the payee. A separation agreement also makes the divorce process through the courts much easier, as it can simply be incorporated into the divorce judgment.

Once the agreement has been worked out to everyone's satisfaction, four original copies of the document are signed by the two lawyers and two spouses. As part of this signing process, you will most often have to also sign a certificate of independent legal advice and an acknowledgment by wife/husband. The certificate declares that your lawyer knows that it was you who signed the document, that she has explained everything in it to you and that you have signed it voluntarily. The acknowledgment affirms that the spouses have consulted with a lawyer, that they know what they are signing and that they are doing it voluntarily.

Setting aside an agreement Separation agreements are not carved in stone and can be changed at a later date, depending on a changing situation or new evidence coming to light. For instance, if it is discovered that one spouse was forced to sign through blackmail or intimidation, the agreement can be overturned. The agreement will also be reconsidered if it is found that it contains false or misleading information or financial omissions.

Courts can and frequently do change separation agreements regarding the amount and length of child support payments and custody and access issues. The same is true of spousal support payments. Many agreements have clauses that include a commitment to revisit certain parts if circumstances change to warrant a review.

But remember, whatever method you use to settle a family law case, always be sure that it meets your needs as much as possible under the circumstances. Fatigue, time, money will all play a role in your decisions, but with the help of a competent lawyer, you should ultimately get an agreement that is fair to both you and your former partner.

Case study: Francine and Nicholas

Francine and Nicholas had been married for 28 years, long enough that the children were grown and their $250,000 home was mostly paid off. Issues of child custody and support were not important since all three children were now in their twenties. Nicholas voluntarily contributed to the university tuition of the last child, so there was no pressing need to get this into a legal agreement.

There were, however, major financial issues in the breakup. Francine had supported John's various careers, sacrificed her own career as a city planner to raise the children and thrown an inheritance of $50,000 into the down payment for their first home. She was working again, now that the children were away from home, but not at a job that paid her well or matched her training.

Nicholas, on the other hand, had done very well in the last few years of business. Two years ago, he had created his own company and was drawing in excess of $150,000 a year. His earning potential was considerably higher; the company itself was probably worth a million dollars, and John had a pension with an actuarial value of $750,000.

Under the *Divorce Act*, the assets acquired during a marriage are divided equally on dissolution – but how can a court easily divide houses, companies and pensions? (This is done quite often in fact but never happily, since it can involve the sale of property or dissolving a good business.)

Through mediation, Francine and Nicholas reached an agreement. Nicholas wanted to keep his pension, so Francine had to receive $375,000 to compensate for that value. She got most of that by keeping the house, and the remainder by taking a 10 percent share in Nicholas's company. As well, Nicholas agreed to provide spousal support for a period of five years of the difference between Francine's salary and the $60,000 a year she would have made as a city planner.

Their lawyers totalled up the financial gains and losses of each side and felt it was close enough to equal division of property. The final agreement easily got court approval.

Chapter Six

Child custody and access

There is little doubt that the most serious consequence of divorce is the emotional, psychological and material effects on the children in the family. The trauma that children experience as a result of divorce can be very serious if the split-up is not approached in an open and direct way, with a lot of support from the family. This is often very difficult for parents to provide when they are experiencing their own hurt and confusion. In many respects, a bitterly contested divorce or separation will only aggravate the negative effects on children.

CUSTODY AND ACCESS

As outlined in the *Divorce Act*, custody and access are related legal terms that concern parenting responsibilities both during and after a legal separation or divorce. The person who is awarded custody, often called the custodial parent, is the person who is legally responsible for the "care, upbringing and any other incident of custody" as it relates to the children. The custodial parent is the person who makes the major decisions concerning health care, education and the general welfare of a child.

Access refers to the visiting rights of the parent who does not have custody of the children. The parent who has access rights, sometimes called the non-custodial parent, has lost all legal guardianship but has the right to be informed about the health, education and welfare of the children. Unfortunately, many non-custodial parents lose their rights to be involved in the decisions affecting the children on these matters.

If non-custodial parents disagree with decisions custodial parents are making about the children, the only way they can affect these decisions is to challenge them in court – a process that is time consuming and expensive, with the outcome always in doubt. Parents with access do have certain limited rights in cases of an emergency, but for the most part they become loving and supportive parents on the sidelines, standing by in case the custodial parent becomes debilitated or dies.

Normally it is the parents of the children who apply for custody and access, although other interested parties can apply as well. The *Divorce Act* specifically says that custody or access can be granted to one or more persons. This enables the courts to give custody and access to either or both parents depending on the circumstances. There can be either **sole** or **joint custody**. It is possible, although rare, that another family member or caregiver can apply for custody or access. People other than the parents need special court permission to intervene in custody and access proceedings.

There is an increasing acceptance by the courts that grandparents have access rights to their grandchildren and can often provide important emotional stability for children going through divorce.

Interim custody and access One of the orders or motions that can be filed with the court before a divorce petition is decided is the granting of an interim order that relates to custody and support. Children need to be taken care of and supported financially while the divorce negotiations and possible trial are proceeding. Usually, the courts will leave the children with the parent with whom they are living at the time divorce proceedings are initiated. The courts are very reluctant to disturb children's lives any more than they already are.

THE BEST INTERESTS OF THE CHILD

When courts try to determine to whom to award custody, the key factor they consider is "the best interests of the child." The *Divorce Act* says that the best interests of the child are to be determined by evaluating the "condition, means, needs and other circumstances" of the child. While these criteria are useful, they are still open to interpretation and in the final analysis can be quite subjective. The federal legislation has outlined some guidelines to help courts determine custody and access. Some of those considerations include

- the physical and emotional well-being and security of the child
- the plans for the education and maintenance of the child as described by the person requesting custody or access
- the financial position of the parents so as to apportion responsibility for support
- the religious and ethical needs of the child
- the moral and ethical standards of the person seeking custody or access according to local community standards
- the sensitivity of the person seeking custody or access as a parent and in particular that person's understanding of the particular needs of the child

The provinces have added further criteria to guide their courts. Ontario has added recommendations that include the emotional ties to various people involved in the affected family, the views and preferences of the child, as well as the length of time a child has lived in a stable environment. In the final analysis, no guidelines can settle these kinds of issues. In recognizing this fact, the *Divorce Act* stresses the importance of using other methods, particularly mediation, to settle custody and access disputes.

Assessment In certain situations, the courts may assign a professional evaluator who interviews the family and makes recommendations to the court. These assessors can be used whether or not the divorcing parents agree to the procedure. What the assessors are looking for when they examine a family situation are the needs of the children and who is providing them. However, the court rarely assigns assessors to a case and only in very difficult and contentious situations.

The physiological parent When making decisions regarding custody, the courts try to identify the person who is the physiological parent. This is basically the parent who spends the most time and effort caring for the child. Traditionally, this has most often been the mother of the child. The courts used to reason that during a child's "tender years," up to about age seven, the child should be with the biological mother, whom they consider to be most capable of taking care of the child. This practice is not applied as much as it used to be, although it is still influential, especially for babies. The courts will also take into consideration that other family members or caregivers, such as a grandparent or even a neighbor, can be the physiological parent as well.

Past and present behavior of the parents The *Divorce Act* also specifies that the past behavior of the parents should have no bearing on who gets custody and access unless it relates to their ability to parent. At one time, if a divorce were based on the grounds of adultery or cruelty, the "guiltless" parent would automatically be accorded custody. What the present ruling suggests is that even if a parent has serious problems with marital relationships, he or she can still be a good parent. Nonetheless, while legislation has moved away from assigning blame in marriage breakups and custody assessments, there are still individual judges who believe that past behavior should be factored into the determination of who gets custody and access.

The courts will also take into consideration which parent is most likely to allow access by the other parent to the children. This is often referred to as the "friendly parent" or "maximum contact" rule. If a judge feels that a parent may be obstructive about providing access to the other parent, the court may award custody to the other parent if he or she appears accommodating about providing access.

The courts will also take into consideration conduct by a parent that may harm a child's emotional, physiological or spiritual welfare. In the case of known physical or sexual abuse, the distinction is quite simple, but the courts will also take into consideration addictions, sexual preferences and relationships with third parties or other behavior the courts think detrimental to a child's welfare.

The courts are also reluctant to disturb the established family dynamic. As a result, they generally consider it important to keep siblings together to provide support and stability for each other during these disruptive times.

Preferences of the children Under certain conditions, the courts will also factor in the desires of the children affected by divorce. This can be a difficult aspect of any assessment as it depends on the age and maturity of the children involved. The courts are well aware that parents can influence their children in deciding whom they want to be with as a result of divorce. In general, the courts will only seriously take into consideration older children in their teens whom they believe are mature enough to make clear decisions about whom they want to be with. The courts are also aware that the older children get, the less influence the courts will have on what they want to do regarding custody and access. In certain difficult cases, one of the parents can request, or the courts can assign, a lawyer to represent children. Lawyers can represent babies right up to children of legal age who are still dependent on their parents for support.

 Parents involved in custody and access disputes should present detailed parenting plans for the short and long term to better enable the courts to make good decisions in these matters.

Although custody and access are the legal terms that are used to deal with parenting issues during and after divorce, many parents and critics of the system have begun to use words like co-parenting, shared parenting or co-operative parenting that suggest that parents have equal responsibility in parenting children who are effected by divorce or separation.

CUSTODY ISSUES

Custody can be further divided into sole custody or joint custody. **Sole custody** is the norm in Canadian courts although they are increasingly being laden with conditions relating to the rights and responsibilities of the person who has access. It is not uncommon for the courts to impose travel and moving restrictions on sole custodial parents. The courts and the non-custodial parent must be informed about moves or travel with the children and there is an opportunity for the non-custodial parent to prevent this from happening. In some cases where custodial parents wish to move to a distant location for a good reason (such as a better job), the courts will grant the request but reduce the support payments from non-custodial parents to compensate for their increased travel costs. In other circumstances, say if there is a legitimate reason to fear that the custodial or non-custodial parent may abduct the children, one parent may be forced to hand over their passports to the court for assurance or make a substantial money deposit in an attempt to guarantee their return.

Joint custody refers to the situation, still quite rare but on the increase, where a court awards custody to both parents who have a co-operative plan to share physical custody and joint decision-making responsibility. Here joint physical custody refers to the situation where the children live more or less equal amounts of time with each parent. During the time the children are with them, each parent has sole custodial responsibility for the children. Joint decision-making responsibility refers to equal authority to make decisions about the important child-rearing tasks like health, education and welfare even though the children may not be living an equal amount of time with each parent. For these arrangements to work, there has to be a high level of co-operation between the caregivers.

Where joint custody is arranged, it is common for the courts to reduce or eliminate child support payments. Some people argue that this is a way for one parent, usually the father, to avoid paying child support. Although this can be the case, on balance the courts see joint custody to be in the best interests of the child.

ACCESS ISSUES

Access refers primarily to the rights of the parent who does not have custody to spend time with the children. Many divorce or separation settlements regarding access state that the non-custodial parent will have reasonable or liberal access to the children. These definitions can work well while there is fairly good communication and co-operation between parents, but they can break down if hostilities develop. If this happens the non-custodial parent may have to ask the courts to enforce these arrangements. As a result, some settlements will specify the exact time the non-custodial parent has a right to be with the children. For instance, a settlement may stipulate that the children are dropped off at a certain location at 6 p.m. every second Friday and will be returned to a specific location at 7 p.m. on Sunday, and that they will have access to the children on alternate birthdays, Christmas and Easter and for a specified time during summer holidays.

Under certain conditions the courts can impose conditions on access by the non-custodial parent. In cases where there have been incidents of hostility or real or potential abuse, the courts can order supervised access. This can mean that a third party, a mutual friend or respected community member, must agree to be present during the exchange of the children or for the entire time the non-custodial parent is with the children.

Physical or sexual abuse One of the most difficult circumstances to deal with is if there has been a history of violence or sexual abuse within a family. Society is slowly realizing the extent and seriousness of this issue and these concerns are beginning to be expressed through the courts. Most professionals and lay people are obliged or encouraged to report cases of child abuse, whether physical or sexual. If child abuse is proved, the offending parent can lose all custody and access rights and be charged with a criminal act with all the force of the law as punishment and can be sued for damages by the child.

In rare cases, accusations of sexual abuse can be false and are used as tactical maneuvers during legal proceedings. As this is a serious offense, parents falsely accusing the other of abuse can lose all rights to custody and access and can be charged with the criminal offense of perjury, which can result in fines or imprisonment.

Paternity Occasionally, it might be necessary to determine the paternity of a child in a divorce case. This means establishing who is the father or mother of a child. The need for this can arise in situations where there is some question about whom the father or mother actually is. There have been a number of cases where teenage children have traced men they believe to be their fathers so they can file for support payments. Some unmarried women have done the same thing to secure support payments for their children. Many provinces have developed guidelines to help the courts determine paternity; if there is still doubt, the courts can order blood testing of the alleged mother and father and the child in question. If the alleged father should refuse to take a blood test, the courts can take this refusal as probable proof that the man is the father. Although blood tests do not provide conclusive proof, they are 95 percent accurate. DNA tests are more conclusive, but they are considerably more expensive.

Case study: Alain and Janice Hutchinson

The Hutchinsons were a model family until the separation. Alain was a good father to his three children – Noah, 12, Martin, 10 and Ellen, eight – and the children adored him. Janice worked part-time as a dental assistant but was always at home when her kids finished their school day. She was a very loving mother. When Alain announced that he was leaving the relationship, Janice was hurt and the children were shocked.

Both Alain and Janice were remarkably fair in dealing with the monetary issues of their separation. The problem came with custody and access. Alain wanted an order for join custody. He had rented a house only a block away from the family home, which Janice was keeping. He thought the kids could spend half their time at his house and half at Janice's.

Janice did not agree. She didn't like Alain's new girlfriend and she knew the long hours that Alain put in at his job. As well, she had been the primary caregiver to the children, handling most of the day-to-day concerns and health and education decisions. She opposed joint custody.

When either party opposes a petition of joint custody, it is impossible for the court to make it work. Alain gave up on his petition and asked, instead, for undefined but liberal access to the kids. Janice wanted something more precise – "there's no way he can just ask for the kids whenever he feels like it" – and replied that she wanted Alain to have specified access of every other weekend, one night per week, two vacation weeks per year and half days at Christmas and Thanksgiving.

Alain was hurt and insulted. He felt that his parenting and commitment weren't being acknowledged by Janice and threatened to delay the divorce until she accommodated him. The wrangle brought them both to a mediator, who helped hammer out an agreement that accepted Janice's terms but added "and other times as negotiated by the parties."

Those other times turned out to be substantial over the years. When Noah was 15, he decided he'd rather live full-time at Alain's house. After Janice moved to a new town to take a job, Martin decided that he, too, would prefer to stay with his dad (and his friends, of course). Janice and Ellen moved with Janice's new partner to a town several hundred kilometres away. There was still some movement of the children back and forth through their teenage years, but no agreement drafted seven years earlier could have anticipated all that.

Chapter Seven

Spousal and child support

After custody and access, the issue of support, particularly child support, is the most important issue in separation and divorce cases.

In all cases where child and spousal support are being claimed, financial statements declaring all assets must be made to the courts. The only circumstances in which financial statements do not have to be submitted is in uncontested divorces where all the property division has been worked out to everyone's satisfaction.

SPOUSAL SUPPORT

Under the *Divorce Act*, there are four main objectives that the courts try to address when ordering support payments to spouses. The spousal support order should

1. recognize any economic advantages or disadvantages to the spouses arising from the marriage or its breakdown
2. apportion between the spouses the financial consequences arising from the care of any child of the marriage
3. relieve any economic hardship of the spouses arising from the breakdown of the marriage
4. insofar as is practical, promote the economic self-sufficiency of each spouse within a reasonable period of time

In considering these four objectives, the federal courts can take into consideration such things as the length of time the spouses lived together, whether the relationship was a traditional "husband works, wife stays home" model or a more modern one and whether there was any prior agreements for spousal support.

In the past the courts tended to apply three methods of arriving at the amount of spousal support. The "income security model" is based on a support obligation because the couple have lived together for a period of time. The "compensatory model" is considered to be compensation from lost income by one of the spouses, most usually the women, who gave up employment opportunities in order to raise the children of the marriage. The "clean break model" is designed to provide spouses with enough financial support so they can become self-supporting.

Today, the two main factors that federal and provincial courts take into consideration when calculating spousal support are the needs of the spouse, usually the wife, and the ability of the other spouse, usually the husband, to pay. *Need and ability to pay are the only considerations.* Increasingly, however, consideration is given to the ability of the wife to support herself.

The amount of spousal support and the length of time support orders will last are determined by the courts based on a variety of factors. The usual payment period is monthly instalments but they can be every week, every six months, or lump-sum payments, depending on the circumstances. For instance, if the court feels that the spouse paying the support may not make regular payments or if there is obvious hostility between the spouses, the court may order a lump-sum payment to come out of any property settlement. If there is no income but there is property, the court may order liquidation the property to generate a lump-sum payment.

Fixed-term or conditional spousal support orders can last for specific periods of time. For instance, a conditional order could last until the partner receiving support remarries, gets retrained or finds full-time employment. Fixed-term payments are becoming increasingly common as the emphasis in the courts is always to get both spouses financially self-sufficient as quickly as possible after marriage breakdown.

Regardless of the objective of both partners becoming self-sufficient, the courts will take into consideration the age of the spouse and the duration of the relationship. For instance, a woman who has been a homemaker in a long-term relationship, and has who has forgone a career, may well get life-long support, especially if she is sick or unable to work. The courts also recognize that women in this situation may not have the necessary skills to find work that maintains a standard of living similar to what they experienced while they were married.

Tax considerations must be factored into support payments as well. Lump-sum support payments are tax-free while periodic payments are taxable income for the person receiving the support and are tax-deductible by the payer of the support.

Another factor to consider is the amount of the property settlement. The larger the property settlement in favor of the spouse requesting support, the lower the spousal support will be.

It is increasingly common for support orders to include a cost of living clause as well. This avoids the repeated inconvenience of having to return to court to have changes made to compensate for loss of support due to inflation.

Spousal conduct The federal *Divorce Act* says the courts will not take into consideration any "misconduct of a spouse in relation to the marriage." This means, for instance, that any adultery or cruelty that may have lead directly to the marriage breakup may not be taken into consideration when a spouse seeks support. This approach is in line with the no-fault bias of the act. However, you should bear in mind that judges are human and lawyers can emphasize the past conduct of a spouse during a trial. Issues of spousal conduct have been known to play a role during decisions about support. For instance, support payments are more likely to be higher for an older woman who is being left by a husband for a younger woman, than for a young woman who is leaving a marriage because she wants to find herself. Past conduct may also influence spouses to negotiate an out-of-court settlement if they do not wish their behavior to be made public during a trial. For public figures and other prominent individuals, a quiet settlement is far more preferable to messy legal wrangling.

A recent survey of divorce gave an overview of the situation and found that

- Two-thirds of divorced women who have custody of children live below the poverty line, and this situation is on the increase.
- The average amount of support per child is declining.
- The higher the income of a man who is providing support payments, the smaller these payments are of his total income.
- Settlements negotiated by lawyers for support tend to be lower than court-awarded support orders.
- Less than 20 percent of wives receive spousal support payments in divorce cases.

Changes to spousal support orders

Either spouse under a spousal support order can apply for alterations, or variations as they are called by the courts, if circumstances change. Factors taken into consideration include whether the supporting spouse is remarrying or is involved in a common-law relationship.

If a spouse receiving support should die, then the support payments are stopped. If the payer should die, the support can still be ordered from the estate if there are the resources to cover the payments.

CHILD SUPPORT

The general principle for child support orders is that the children should have a standard of living similar to what they had before the marriage broke up. In making its decisions, the court takes into consideration the "needs, means, condition and any other circumstance that affect the well-being of the child." This is a highly laudable goal. Unfortunately, what usually happens when a marriage breaks up, particularly where there are children involved, is that all parties become poorer. The reason for this is quite simple. In many cases when a couple breaks up, two households have to be maintained (with rent, utilities, transportation, food, etc.) by the same income. Even when both spouses are working, two separate households cost more to run than one.

 Support and visitation are two separate legal issues. A non-custodial parent paying support, for instance, cannot withhold payments if the custodial parent withholds access, or if the children behave poorly or have a hostile attitude. In other words, child support payments are not dependent on the good behavior of the custodial parent or the children.

In determining child support, the courts include these considerations:

1. Both spouses have a joint financial obligation to maintain the child.
2. This obligation is apportioned between the spouses according to their relative abilities to contribute to the performance of the obligation.
3. Because children are not to blame for their parents' divorce, they should be able to enjoy the same standard of living as they would have enjoyed if the marriage had not broken down.
4. Maintaining separate households with no corresponding increase in income usually precludes the children from enjoying their previous standard of living. Their rights of support should, nevertheless, take priority over those of either parent.
5. The parent with whom the children continue to live may indirectly benefit from the non-custodial parent's payment of child support. This may be inevitable, though, if the law is to achieve the goal of protecting the financial interests of the children.

In arriving at the appropriate support payment, the courts must leave each parent with enough resources to meet their own needs. Support payments, for instance, cannot force the payer onto social assistance.

AMOUNT OF SUPPORT

Child support guidelines In 1997, the Federal Child Support Guidelines came into effect and have made it easier to calculate the amount of child support paid by a non-custodial parent. These guidelines are more or less mandatory, although the courts do have some discretion in applying them, depending on the circumstances.

The federal guidelines on child support are quite complex and perhaps best left to your lawyer. Still, if you go to the Department of Justice Web site at **canada.justice.ca** and follow the links, you'll find dollar figures for various income levels in the different provincial jurisdictions. As a rough guide, here are the national figures for the end of the year 2000.

Yearly income	Monthly payment by number of children		
	One child	*Two children*	*Three children*
$28,000	$252	$424	$561
$33,400	$294	$488	$644
$44,000	$381	$624	$818
$50,000	$429	$700	$917

The guidelines were introduced in order to

* ensure fairness and consistency in child support payments
* reduce the likelihood of conflict between the parties
* provide a quicker, less costly way of resolving differences

The formula works by matching up the income range of non-custodial parents and the number of children involved. The custodial parent's income is not used in the calculations at all. The formula is adjusted accordingly for parents who have joint or split custody of their children. If the custodial parent has a limited income and will suffer undue hardship as a result of following the formula, the courts will make adjustments. This formula only applies to support payments arrived at since 1997. However, guidelines may apply to support payments arrived at before that date, if variances are later being requested of the court.

Although there are specific guidelines for each province, the courts have some discretionary powers to determine the amount of child support. The factors they can take into consideration can be very extensive. Aside from the normal expenses of accommodation, food, clothes, education and child care, they can include extra educational classes, hobby expenses, family vacations, camp expenses, sports equipment and even special religious education. In spite of what a court may consider in calculating support payments, the overriding criteria is the non-custodial parent's ability to pay.

In calculating the amount of support payments, the courts consider the basic needs of the paying parent, but the priority is always on ensuring the child support. Courts consider support payments more of a priority than car payments or bank loans. To use a popular expression, it is always "kids over cars."

Payments can also vary depending on whether there is split custody (when parents each have one or more of the children) or joint custody (where parents have the children about an equal amount of time). Settlements usually include cost-of-living allowances.

Non-biological parents can be required to pay support as well. If a spouse has been acting as a parent, legally or informally, the non-biological stepparent can be required to pay support payments if he or she has been acting as a parent to the child during the relationship. For example, although the natural father is considered by the courts to be responsible for the support of his child, the natural father may not be present or in a position to provide any support. In such a situation, the courts will require the non-biological father to provide some support.

Payment schedules By far the most common way to make support payments is on a monthly basis. The courts can order payments to be made weekly or according to any other schedule they think appropriate given the circumstances. Occasionally the courts order lump-sum child support. For instance, if the courts believe the payer may leave the country or will attempt to dispose of assets, or if the nature of the payer's income justifies it, the courts can order a lump-sum payment. It may have to do with a lump-sum payment of arrears or special needs like orthodontics, or may be because the court believes the non-custodial parent will not pay periodic orders.

Enforcement Only parents can make claims for child support payments. After support payments have been established, children of legal age can apply to the courts to change or enforce support payments if the need arises.

Length of support payments Most legislation makes support payments mandatory until the child reaches the age of 16 or until the child is no longer financially dependent on the parent. In reality this gives the court considerable leeway in determining the duration of child support. If a child is disabled or has a long-term illness, support payments can go on for the life of the child, depending on the circumstances. It is also increasingly common for courts to award support to children who wish to continue their education into university. The usual practice is to award the support up until the first university degree.

Contentious issues in child support

You don't want to go back to court to clarify every issue that comes up with child support. Of course, every divorce situation is different, but here are the usual ways to handle some common contentious issues:

- **Custodial parent is away** Child support does not end (or even get prorated) if the non-custodial parent voluntarily agrees to look after the children for a period of time. (After all, rent, heat and electrical bills don't stop when a child is with the other parent.)
- **Vacation** Child support continues even if the children are taking an agreed-on holiday with the non-custodial parent (unless you both have agreed otherwise).
- **School costs** Ordinary school costs for books and clothing should be covered by the regular child support payments. A special trip or activity, however, should be shared equally by the parents.
- **School and university tuition** Unless negotiated in the agreement, there are no established guidelines.
- **Braces, dental work and special medical costs** As with other one-time, special situations, these costs should be shared.
- **Ballet lessons, summer camps, etc.** Unless the non-custodial spouse agrees to pay half, these must be handled by the custodial parent.

Child support payments can be stopped if the child has "voluntarily withdrawn from parental control" and is no longer considered a "child of the marriage." This means that if a child over 16 voluntary leaves home and is not going to school, child support payments can be stopped. It also means that children over 16 cannot leave home voluntarily and then easily apply to the courts for support from their parents. The courts will, however, issue support orders to children over 16 who have been forced to move in with other family members or friends if they have left the family home as a result of sexual abuse or domestic violence.

Changes to child support orders Courts refer to support order changes as variances or recissions. As with spousal support orders, the courts recognize life changes affecting the financial needs of parents with children. People lose or change their jobs or become ill, and children grow up. While children are young, their expenses are relatively lower than when they are teenagers.

Another common reason for adjusting payments is that divorced people often remarry. Starting new families or marrying into pre-established ones always alters the financial situation and courts are sensitive to these changing needs. Each case is judged on its own merit.

Chapter Eight

Dividing your property

Since this is the most obvious economic aspect of marriage, the courts tend to treat property division in a very businesslike manner. Each spouse brings assets and liabilities to the relationship and builds on them while they are together, but all are divided equally when a marriage breaks up. Property rights for common-law spouses are much more difficult to determine (see Chapter 9), but the principle of equal division of property is very strong for couples who have been married for any length of time. Although the courts try to divide property equally, they are also concerned with dividing equitably all the value of assets a couple have acquired since they married up until the time they separated.

Division of property as a result of divorce or separation is the exclusive jurisdiction of provincial and territorial laws. In these cases the courts always consider the question of property division first. This is done because the amount of property and the way it is divided will have a direct impact on awards of child support and especially spousal support.

Because property can cover a wide variety of assets from objects like houses to future income like pensions, it is very important that you consult a knowledgeable lawyer to look after your interests property division proceedings.

FINANCIAL STATEMENTS

Carefully prepared financial statements are of central importance when dealing with property division. The courts rely on these documents in making decisions. For this reason they must be as complete and thorough as possible. The courts take a dim view of incomplete financial statements and you risk losing credibility if you do not keep financial statements current during the trial. In any case, the opposing lawyer will have the opportunity to cross-examine you during the discovery about your financial statements, so it pays to be as honest and as thorough as you can from the beginning. You are responsible for compiling all the documentation required to support your property claims.

If you have concerns about your financial statements being made public, some provinces will allow them to be kept confidential to the court only.

HOW IS PROPERTY VALUE DETERMINED?

The definition of the kinds of property that can be considered for division during a divorce or separation varies from province to province. Some provinces have two categories: family assets are property that is in general use by the family such as homes, furnishings, savings, family cars, etc; non-family assets are property that is not used by the whole family such as business interests of the spouses, inheritances and awards. Assets specifically allocated to a particular spouse in a marriage contract are exempt from consideration in property division.

Determining the value of property can be difficult for a number of reasons. First, the two of you may value joint property differently, depending on what you intend to do with the property. Consider the situation where a couple jointly owns a business that is valuated at $100,000 by one spouse and at $500,000 by the other. The first valuation is based on the business continuing as a business, while the second is based on selling the property where the business is located to a developer who wants to construct an apartment building. Both parties are right in their own way, as the valuation depends on how you treat the property. Some provinces get around this by using a calculation known as fair market value, while other provinces have not set guidelines and decide each case on its own merits. Other difficult issues are tax considerations in selling or transferring property as well as whether to include real estate commission costs in property sales.

The principle process used by all the provinces in determining property settlements is to add up the value of the property, subtract the debts against the assets and then divide the remaining net value between the parties. Net worth in this case means what is left of the value of a property after any outstanding debts or loans are paid out. For instance, if a house is worth $150,000 but has a $100,000 mortgage still to pay, then after that mortgage is paid off, the remaining $50,000 is divided between the spouses.

All things being more or less the same, the courts try to divide the remaining assets *equally*. However all jurisdictions have the power to divide the property *equitably* as well as equally. Each province recognizes that there may be situations where dividing the property equally between the two spouse would not be fair. A recent court decision in Ontario awarded the matrimonial home to the wife who had bought and paid for it entirely on her own during the course of the marriage. The husband had not worked during the marriage and had contributed nothing to the upkeep or maintenance of the property. In this case the courts decided it would be unfair to award half the house to the husband and gave it all to the wife.

Different provinces take different approaches to this discretionary power. Some provinces will only divide equitably if it would be grossly unfair to divide equally. Other provinces have a much more liberal interpretation of what constitutes unfair and make judgments accordingly.

An exception to this general practice is that Ontario does not make any distinction between various kinds of assets. So all property possessed by a couple, except in some narrow circumstances, are divided on the same basis when a marriage breaks down.

It is also possible and advisable to obtain an order from the court to prevent either spouse from dealing with property they own until the outcome of the negotiations or court proceedings. This is to ensure that the value or ownership of the property remains as it was at the moment of separation. It also ensures that there is property or assets available to settle final judgments at the end of a trial.

Payment of property settlements can either be in the form of a cash settlement based on the net value of the property, or there can be a transfer of title of a specific asset or assets that equal the amount of the judgment.

THE MATRIMONIAL HOME

In all provinces the matrimonial home gets special consideration in the case of legal marriage breakup. All jurisdictions prevent a spouse from selling or mortgaging the matrimonial home without the consent of the other spouse. One of the reasons for doing this is to protect each spouse and the value of the property should the marriage break down.

Most provinces also stipulate equal ownership of the family home in the event of a marriage breakdown no matter who has possession of the matrimonial home at the time of the separation. This also means that either spouse can apply to the courts for possession of the family home. The exceptions are Alberta, British Columbia and Quebec, which do not give this automatic right to possession of the matrimonial home.

PENSIONS

In many provinces pensions are considered assets and can be divided between the spouses when they divorce or separate. The determination of the division varies from province to province and depends on the terms of the specific pension plan. Factors that are considered when evaluating a pension are tax consequences, interest rates, indexing and early retirement provisions. The divisible part of the pension only includes the portion of the pension from the beginning to the end of the marriage.

The Canada Pension Plan (CPP) includes a scheme that provides for the sharing of pension credits accumulated by both spouses while they were married or living in a common-law relationship. The credits for each spouse are totalled together and then each spouse is awarded half. One of the objectives of this credit sharing is to ensure that a spouse who has been a homemaker during the marriage and who has no CPP will receive some pension income in the event the marriage or relationship breaks up.

Evaluating pension plans can be a complex and difficult process and requires professional evaluators to do the job. These professionals can also be expensive, so get a sense from your lawyer about what is involved in your particular situation and how much an evaluation will cost. Make sure that what you might get is more than what you are going to pay for having the pension evaluated.

Case study: Barbara and David

Barbara and David were married for seven years before they split up. During that time, David received an expensive car from his father which he thought was "his," but the laws of Ontario were clear – it became a joint asset of the couple. Similarly, Barbara's father had given them the down payment for their house and the mortgage had been paid out of Barbara's salary, so she thought of the house as "hers." Once again, the house simply becomes a joint asset at the time of divorce.

Both David and Barbara had accumulated some pension credits where they worked. Only those credits during the time of their marriage were considered, but David's higher salary meant that his pension and CPP credits were much higher. Regardless, these were divided equally.

Here's what their assets looked like in a simplified chart:

Property item	Assets	Debts
Family home	$350,000	$177,000 (mortgage)
"Barb's" car	$7,000	
"David's" car	$28,000	$22,000 (car loan)
Chattels (furniture, etc.)	$14,000	
Credit card debt		$3,000
David's pension & CPP	$128,000	
Barb's pension & CPP	$44,000	
RSPs, savings, cash	$34,000	
Totals	**$605,000**	**$202,000**

David and Barbara each had slightly over $200,000 in assets after liabilities, a figure which came as a surprise to both of them. David decided to deed the family home to Barbara to avoid having to come up with a lump sum to compensate for his higher pension credits.

This situation is quite common in households where one spouse earns considerably more or has worked longer than the other. The greater the disparity, the greater the cash transfer on divorce.

Chapter Nine

Common-law relationships

An increasing number of Canadians are living together without getting formally married.

This arrangement is referred to as living common-law and is generally accepted to mean that two people of the opposite sex are living together as husband and wife but are not legally married.

A recent decision by the Supreme Court of Canada makes it illegal to discriminate against homosexual or lesbian couples, or same-sex couples as they are know in law, who are living together in a common-law relationship. Provincial governments are presently adjusting their family laws to conform to this new ruling. When this process is complete, it will mean that same-sex couples will be treated the same as opposite sex couples in common-law relationships when they break up.

As the *Divorce Act* only applies to legally married people, common-law couples are not covered under this federal legislation. However, provincial and territorial family law legislation does make provisions for common-law spouses who are separating. As these laws vary considerably from jurisdiction to jurisdiction, it is very important that you consult a lawyer where you live if you are living common-law and are considering separating.

Some of the criteria the provincial courts use to define common-law spouses are outlined in the table on the next page:

Jurisdiction	Criteria for common-law spouses
NWT, Alberta, Quebec, PEI	No common-law spouse entitlement to support
British Columbia	Two years of living together
Saskatchewan	Three years of living together, or a child and a relationship of some permanence
Manitoba	Five years of living together and substantial dependence between the people involved, or one year of living together with a child
Ontario	Three years of living together, or a relationship of some permanence with a child
New Brunswick	Three years of living together and substantial dependence
Nova Scotia	One year of living together
Yukon	A relationship of some permanence

In determining whether a couple's relationship is legally common-law, the courts tend to use the following guidelines:

- Did they have a sexual relationship?
- Did they share the same accommodation?
- Did they share household expenses?
- Did one partner perform domestic services for the other?
- Were they husband and wife for all intents and purposes?

CHILDREN

Once the courts have established that a relationship is common-law, then the custody and access issues are decided by provincial and territorial family laws that apply to legally married couples. Custody issues are determined by the best interests of the child and access arrangements are decided at the same time. As with children of formal marriages, children of common-law relationships are also legally entitled to financial support when a common-law relationship breaks down. In some cases, even children brought into the marriage by one partner may be entitled to support from the other.

SUPPORT AND PROPERTY DIVISION

In most provincial and territorial jurisdictions where common-law relationships are recognized and where there is a clear need, the courts will award support payments to one party or the other. The amount of support is more or less the same as that awarded to married spouses who qualify (see Chapter 7).

In many jurisdictions this entitlement also applies to a deceased partner's estate. The surviving partner of a common-law relationship can apply to the estate of the deceased partner for support.

Property   Property is the most difficult aspect of separation between common-law couples. Contrary to popular belief, the only property that a common-law spouse can legally claim at separation is property that is clearly identifiable as his or hers. Most often this will be property acquired before the relationship began and brought into the relationship.

But what happens if a couple acquires property while they are living together? This is where separation can get complicated. The general guidelines that the courts have developed to sort out property issues for separating common-law spouses are these:

- Each case is considered a unique case.
- The length of time the couple have been together is considered.
- Courts determine a fair division of property based on the contributions of each spouse.
- A gift from one spouse to the other is seen as the exclusive property of the receiver of the gift and is not subject to division.

While the courts will allow spouses to claim property that they brought into the relationship or acquired personally only during the relationship, the courts will not allow one spouse to become "unjustly enriched" at the expense of the other. This means if one spouse helped the other spouse acquire property and gave up something he or she wanted to do in the process, the courts will try and remedy the situation when the couple separates. The courts have developed a concept known as "constructive trust," which means that the spouse who has the property, say a car registered to one owner, is holding part of the value of the property "in trust" for the other spouse. For instance, if a common-law wife gave up a career to stay home and raise the children while the husband went out and developed a well-paid career that allowed him to buy a cottage, the courts would consider that the husband was holding part of the value of the cottage for his common-law spouse.

This guideline applies to all kinds of property acquired during the relationship. What the courts try to do is determine the intention and motivation for the purchase of the property and then attempt to make an equitable split.

If you have to go to court, it is important to find evidence of *intention* and *contribution* for the courts to make informed decisions. Because of the difficulty of estimating common-law spouses' contributions in property division disputes, the spouses can experience rough justice from the courts. As always, it is better for you and your partner to work out your own arrangements.

Special mention needs to made about CPP benefits. The *CPP Act* states that any people of the opposite sex who have lived together for a minimum of a year and who have separated for over a year, are entitled to a share of the pension credits of the other party. So where one spouse has worked and the other has not, the spouse who has not accumulated any pension credits can apply for a share of the other spouse's pension credits, depending on the length of the relationship.

 The best advice for couples who are living common-law is to develop a written understanding of how property will be divided in the case of death or separation.

Chapter Ten

Enforcing court orders

It is one thing to receive a court order pertaining to a divorce or separation agreement or judgment. It is quite another to have court orders respected by spouses. Let's look at some difficulties that can arise either during or after your legal divorce or separation.

Non-cohabitation or exclusive possession orders It is possible for a couple to share the matrimonial home for some time while they are going through a separation or divorce. The courts will grant temporary possession of the home to both parties as long as it is assured that both parties are genuinely living separate lives with minimal contact. Emotionally, this situation is difficult to maintain and the usual practice is for one partner to leave and find accommodation elsewhere.

In the case of family violence, especially if there are children involved, the courts can grant exclusive possession of the matrimonial home to the victim, usually the wife. The courts recognize that family violence directed at one parent, at each other or at children is very damaging to everyone involved. In this situation, exclusive possession usually means the other partner is not allowed in the home without the express permission of the spouse who is in the family home. The courts will take many factors, such as convenience and the availability of alternatives, into consideration when considering exclusive possession. Some provinces have escalating penalties for partners who violate exclusive orders for possession, with fines to imprisonment for repeated offenses.

Exclusive possession orders are usually temporary orders that last until a settlement is reached or a judgment is made in court. In some cases, the order might be extended longer, for instance, until to the end of the school year, so as not to disrupt the lives of children. What usually happens is that the final judgment is to sell the family home. The courts try to avoid possession being used as a tactical ploy in property or custody disputes.

Personal restraining or non-molestation orders The family law courts can also issue restraining or non-molestation orders, if need be, to prevent a spouse, usually the man, from annoying, harassing or molesting a wife or children. In urgent cases, this order can be granted without the knowledge of the offending spouse. (The order can be challenged by the accused spouse at a later time.)

A non-molestation order can prohibit a spouse from any contact at any time, or limit the contact to specific times and circumstances. For instance, it might allow the father to contact the children on Sunday evenings from 7 to 9 p.m. under the supervision of a third party.

If there has been a history of violence, the Criminal Code can be used to issue a peace bond. This is similar to a civil restraining order, but offenders have to put up money, often $1,000, to ensure they do not break the bond. The advantage of the peace bond for victims is that it costs them nothing and offenders must hire a lawyer to defend themselves in court. In the civil procedure the person seeking the restraining order has to initiate the process, hire a lawyer and pursue the case and enforcement. If not used appropriately, a peace bond can escalate hostilities between former spouses, since it can lead to criminal conviction and a criminal record.

Penalties for breaking a non-molestation order are quite severe and can range from a heavy fine to imprisonment for a first a offense. Police are also authorized to make an arrest without a warrant if they believe such an order has been disobeyed. For this reason, a spouse who has taken out a non-molestation order against a partner should have a number of copies of the order in various locations for easy access in an emergency.

Spouses who are physically violent with their spouses or children can be prosecuted under the Criminal Code. It is increasingly common for courts to award financial compensation to wives and children who have been physically abused by a husband or father. If he cannot pay, the victims have a right to apply to the Criminal Injuries Compensation Board for damages. Even spousal harassment and invasion of privacy are being recognized as grounds for criminal and civil action.

Using the police

In the past, the police have been reluctant to intervene in domestic disputes, believing that marital and divorce issues should be dealt with elsewhere. Fortunately, this approach has changed. Today, in a case where court orders or even personal agreements are being violated and you feel threatened or intimidated, your first move should be this: **call the police**. This advice is as true for a wife whose separated husband is pounding on the door demanding access to her apartment as it is for a dad whose divorced wife is denying him access to the children.

Most large police departments will dispatch a car with a male and a female officer. They have been trained on how to deal with and defuse domestic disputes. However, the police are not lawyers or judges – they can only act on the information that you provide for them. The police cannot solve your divorce issues, but they can make sure that you're safe and the decisions of the courts are obeyed.

Custody concerns The most difficult problems in many cases of separation and divorce are custody and access issues. Most temporary agreements specify certain periods of time when the non-custodial parent can spend time with the children of the marriage. Sadly, these conditions are often ignored – either the non-custodial parent fails to appear at the agreed-on times or demands access at times that are not convenient. Any disagreements on these issues can be devastating to kids, especially so if arguments are carried out in front of them.

The best solution to such issues is, of course, co-operation. If your regular access time begins Friday at 5 p.m., and you're held up at work, call your ex-partner. If you are the ex-partner, don't assume that the non-custodial parent has defaulted on access time because he or she is a few minutes late. A year or two after the divorce is finished, both of you will want some flexibility in negotiating weekends, holidays and vacation times. While a separation or divorce order is usually quite explicit in detailing access, real-life arrangements with kids will always be more complex.

Another issue arises with the older child who says he or she doesn't want to see the non-custodial parent. This requires delicate negotiation. If you are the custodial parent, you don't want to be seen as interfering with your child's relationship with your ex-partner, but you can't really compel a child to do something against his or her wishes. Sometimes it's best to encourage your child to talk directly to the other parent, and get yourself out of the middle.

Remember, the healthiest scenario for children is having two parents who continue to love and look after them even though the parents live apart. For your children's sake, co-operation is so much more sensible than arguments. After all, you probably ended the relationship so your children wouldn't have to face that on a day-to-day basis. Why bring it back after the divorce?

The non-custodial parent must remember that access and support issues are not connected except on the paper of your divorce or separation agreement. If you are having problems getting access to the kids when you want it, you still have no justification to cut support payments. For immediate access problems, call the police. For repeated access problems, go back to the courts.

While many custodial parents worry about the cases of child abduction that are reported in the press, this is really a very minor concern in Canada. Millions of Canadian children are living with a custodial parent, fewer than 50 are abducted per year, according to police statistics. Of course, it is a criminal offense to abduct a child under a custody order if the intent is to deprive the custodial parent of the child. This is why a child travelling across the Canadian border with one parent will need a letter from the other parent to assure customs officials that an abduction is not taking place. The penalty for child abduction by a non-custodial parent is up to 10 years in prison.

Support payment orders At the present time, research indicates that between 30 and 50 percent of support orders are not fully honored. These figures include late and partial payments, but up to 30 percent of non-custodial parents, mainly men, do not pay support orders at all.

Enforcing court orders can be difficult both in terms of the time, energy and money involved in getting the defaulting ex-partner to pay up.

Until recently, it was up to creditors (the parents owed the support payments) to pursue the matter at their own expense if support orders were not paid. They had to hire a lawyer to take their case to court, with all the additional costs and delays this produced. In many cases, chasing support money was more trouble and expense than it was worth. Recently the federal government and many provinces have set up support enforcement programs that take on the responsibility of pursuing parents who are avoiding paying support. Although information gathered by these programs is confidential, it can be exchanged between agencies under a court order.

The most common way for these agencies to enforce support orders is to garnishee wages. The agencies can garnishee up to 50 percent of the defaulter's wages to pay support and can do this on an ongoing basis. This amount is remitted to the agency by the debtor's employer and then is sent on to the creditor. The agencies will only send what they receive, so if they only receive partial payment, this is what is sent. If they cannot collect anything, they are unable to send anything to the creditor. Co-operation between federal and provincial governments also allows agencies to garnishee income such as tax refunds, CPP benefits and other benefits.

If your ex-partner has property, it is also possible for the agency to put a writ of execution or warrant of distress against the property. The property, which can include land, cars and bank accounts, can be sold or liquidated to pay the support debt. This is an effective way of ensuring payment, but if your ex-partner is serious about not paying, he or she can often find ways to protect property against such actions.

Theoretically, the courts can also imprison debtors for non-payment. This is rarely used unless the debtor is more than able to pay but wilfully refuses to do so. However, some provinces will revoke drivers' licenses for non-payment of arrears.

Most provinces have maintenance enforcement programs that have the responsibility of locating support payment debtors. These programs are administered under the justice departments in each province or territory. Further information can be obtained from the federal Child Support Information Line at 1-888-373-2222.

Enforcing property orders Property orders are relatively simple to carry out if you and your ex-partner were married. At the end of a trial a judge can determine how the award is to be paid. If the wife is awarded a specific sum of money, then the courts can insist that property be liquidated to cover the money. This enables the couple to settle the situation right away and avoid problems down the road.

If this method of dividing property was not dealt with at the time of judgment, it can still be done at a later date. Unfortunately, the longer the delay, the more difficult it becomes to collect. Your lawyer, for instance, can issue a writ of execution on property to prevent it being sold until the debt is paid off, or on property to be liquidated to cover property orders. Also wages and other income can be garnisheed to pay for property orders if there is no longer any property to divide.

Contempt When court orders are wilfully disregarded, the legal system falls into "disrepute," which is referred to as contempt of court. Since this is seen as weakening or undermining the authority and credibility of the law, the courts can be strict in dealing with people who are in contempt. Contempt findings are most often used during court proceedings to ensure that proper procedure and decorum are maintained. However, they can be declared by judges at any time they feel appropriate. The punishment can be a fine, imprisonment or a refusal to hear a case. In court this can be used effectively to prevent a person in contempt from filing orders with the court. In extreme cases, a judge could throw out the case of a person who is in contempt and award the other party complete judgment for their claim.

An action for contempt of court can also be put before a judge by a lawyer who is trying to enforce a court order that is being ignored by a spouse in a family law settlement. Because a judge can put someone in jail for disobeying a court order, the criteria for contempt is quite rigorous. This power is only used to deal with a flagrant disregard of court orders.

Chapter Eleven

Moving on

While you are in the midst of a separation and divorce, it may seem as if this time of grief and turmoil will never end. You seem to spend much of your time and energy dealing with your lawyer, the children, your soon-to-be ex-partner and your own sadness. Without doubt, a divorce is a very difficult time, one that will take you through the predictable stages of depression, anger, resentment and, finally, resigned acceptance.

But through all this, you must remember that you do have a future, that this time of stress will end soon enough. In a year, or two, or three, both you and your ex-partner will be moving on to new lives. There may be new relationships and, for 60 percent of divorced people, there will be new partnerships as well. The pain of this divorce will largely be over and you'll be dealing with a new kind of life.

Nonetheless, your years of marriage and any children from it will remain issues to be dealt with. By the second or third year after divorce, most custody and access arrangements have settled into a routine, but there may still be job moves and vacation opportunities that neither of you anticipated. Teenage children frequently assert their right to live where they want, exclusively, or to ignore one parent or the other with seeming impunity. Their behavior is not a function of divorce, but the breakup and confused patterns of parenting that often follow separation or divorce seem to make things worse. Try to keep a steady hand as your children go through their own predictable phases of adolescence.

You will also find your own life changing as new career opportunities come your way. The spousal support that seemed so important for a while may become trivial. You may find that your financial circumstances become quite the reverse of what they were at the breakup, with your ex-partner perhaps in a much more difficult spot. That, of course, is not your problem anymore.

The biggest challenge you'll likely face comes when a new partner arrives in your life. Then you'll have to face introductions to the children, their acceptance or hostility to your new friend and all the questions of forming partnerships that become more complex as the years go on. Often, your ex-spouse will be dealing with the same issues. You both have a choice in these matters. You can be cold, hostile or uncommunicative with each other – and have your children pick up your attitudes in most unpleasant ways. Or you can be reasonable and civil to each other, negotiating new territory as it appears. Without any doubt, a friendly divorce is better than one marked by acrimony. There is much to be said for simply being polite, if not gracious.

Ten or 20 years from now, when child support and access issues are a dim memory, your children will be graduating, getting married and having children of their own. You and your ex-partner will be in the same convocation hall, the same church, the same hospital visiting room. Surely it would be better if you could both smile, exchange the news and share the joy of your children's accomplishments. Many, divorced couples find themselves able to do this. The sooner you and your partner manage to reach this stage, the better for all concerned.

Appendix One

Glossary

Access The opportunity to visit with a child not in your custody. Under the terms of the *Divorce Act*, a spouse exercising access rights is also entitled to information about the child's health, welfare and education, unless a court orders otherwise.

Adultery Sexual intercourse by a husband or wife with someone of the opposite sex who is not his or her spouse.

Affidavit A typed, sworn statement, signed by a person involved in legal proceedings. It is witnessed by someone else and presented to the court in support of a motion.

Appeal When a person affected by a judge's decision believes that the judge has made a mistake, the person can ask a higher court to review the decision. The higher court can uphold, change or send the decision back to the original court for reconsideration.

Arbitration A third party is asked to decide a case for two people who cannot agree. This person acts as a "private" judge with rules and procedures made to the liking of the parties involved.

Child The *Divorce Act* defines a "child of the marriage" as a child of both spouses, a child of one of the spouses toward whom the other spouse acts as a parent, or a child toward whom both spouses act as a parent. Biological children, adopted children and children looked after by the spouses may all be considered children of the marriage.

Collusion An agreement or conspiracy to fabricate or suppress evidence or to deceive the court.

Condonation The forgiving of a matrimonial offense with full knowledge of the circumstances, followed by an acceptance of the offending spouse back into the family.

Connivance The marital misconduct of one spouse caused by, or knowingly permitted by, the other spouse.

Constructive trust A term used by the courts to designate that part of the value of property owned by one spouse in a common-law relationship is held "in trust" for the other spouse.

Common-Law spouse A person with whom someone of the opposite sex, or the same sex, is living with as a partner but to whom he or she is not legally married.

Confidentiality People in certain situations are protected by law from having to give any evidence in court regarding communication between them. Communication between lawyers and clients have this special protection.

Contempt of court A method used to control what happens in court. If someone wilfully disobeys an order given by a judge, or acts in such a way as to bring disrepute to the legal system, a judge can impose a fine or prison sentence.

Contested divorce If either the husband or wife disputes the grounds for divorce, or if the spouses are unable to agree on child or spousal support arrangements, then the courts are asked to impose a solution.

Costs Sums payable for legal services. When matters are contested in court, a judge has the discretion to order that the losing party pay a portion of the successful party's legal costs. In most divorce cases today, both sides pay their own costs.

Discovery One of the steps in legal proceedings where lawyers ask the opposing party questions related to the content of affidavits and pleadings.

Divorce Termination of the legal relationship of marriage between a husband and wife.

Divorce petition The first official court document submitted by a spouse who is seeking a divorce.

Domestic violence The use of force, either real or threatened, by a spouse against the other spouse or property.

Garnishee A legal procedure that allows for the seizure of money owing to a person who has not paid a court-ordered debt.

Interim orders There may be a considerable period between the initial filing of a divorce application and the date at which a court is able to grant a divorce and related support, custody and access orders. On request, a court can make a temporary order for the interim period to stabilize custody or access arrangements, or to provide financial support for a spouse or child.

Joint petition An arrangement by which a mother and a father can continue to share responsibility for making major decisions that affect their children, regardless of which parent the child lives with on a day-to-day basis.

Judgment The final decision rendered by a judge on any issue put before the court during the course of a trial.

Litigation The process of resolving a dispute through the legal system.

Marriage The voluntary union for life of one man and one woman to the exclusion of all others. In Canada, couples are required to go through a civil or religious ceremony to comply with provincial or territorial laws where the marriage takes place.

Marriage breakdown The sole ground for legally ending a marriage under the terms of the *Divorce Act*. Marriage breakdown can be established in three ways: through evidence that one spouse committed adultery or committed physical or mental cruelty, or that the spouses intentionally lived separate and apart for at least one year.

Matrimonial home The place of residence of the married couple. Common-law couples do not have a matrimonial home, according to the law, as they are not legally married.

Mediation A process by which, with the aid of a neutral third party, people in situations of conflict or potential conflict attempt to resolve their differences and reach a mutually acceptable agreement.

Minutes of settlement A signed document setting out how the parties in a legal dispute agree to have their conflict resolved.

Motion A request to the court, accompanied by an affidavit, for a temporary order such as interim custody or support.

Offer to settle An informal or formal offer to settle disputes in divorce or separation proceedings.

Order A decision make by a judge in a matter that the court has been asked to resolve.

Parties The spouses or anyone else involved in a case before the courts.

Petition for divorce A formal document presented to a court with which a person asks the court to dissolve his or her marriage.

Pleadings All the official documents submitted to a court describing each person's claim in a family law case.

Reasons for judgment A written rationale produced by a judge to explain the reasons, based in legislation and precedent, for decisions in a divorce or separation case.

Restraining order A court order that prevents one spouse from contacting the other, or that limits access to children of the relationship.

Retainer The contract and money advance by which a lawyer is hired to take a case.

Rules of procedure The procedure that lawyers must follow to take a case through the civil justice system.

Separate To stop living together as man and wife with the intention of ending the relationship.

Separation agreement A signed contract between the parties to a divorce or separation that documents resolved differences of custody and access, spousal and child support, division of property and other matters.

Shared parenting A term used to describe a sharing of the responsibility in making decisions regarding important issues affecting the raising of children.

Spousal support An amount of money paid by one spouse to another. It can be paid in a lump sum or on a regular basis and can go on for a fixed period or indefinitely.

Spouse A word used to describe each partner in a married or common-law relationship.

Statutory Allowed or required by legislation.

Uncontested divorce If neither the husband nor the wife disputes the grounds for divorce, and if they are able to reach an agreement regarding child care and financial arrangements, it may be possible to ask a judge to grant a divorce without a lengthy court hearing.

Variation If the circumstances of a particular support, custody or access order change, a person affected by the order can ask a judge to alter the order to make it fit the new circumstances.

Bibliography

Dealing with Divorce: Your Rights and Responsibilities, by Julien D. Payne and Marilyn A. Payne, McGraw-Hill Ryerson, 1991.

Divorce Guide for Ontario: Your Own Step-by-Step Guide for Obtaining a Divorce, by Sandra J. Meyrick, International Self-Council Press Ltd., 1996.

For the Sake of the Children, by Kris Kline and Stephen Pew, Prima Publishing, 1991.

In the Name of the Fathers: The Story behind Child Custody, by Susan Crean, Amanita Enterprises, 1998.

Our Turn: The Good News about Women and Divorce, Christopher Hayes, Deborah Anderson and Melinda Blau, Pocket Books/Simon & Schuster, 1993.

Putting Children First: A Guide for Parents Breaking Up, by Hanna McDonough and Christina Bartha, University of Toronto Press, 1999.

Surviving Your Parent's Divorce: A Guide for Young Canadians, by Michael G. Cochrane, Prentice Hall Canada Inc., 1995.

Surviving Your Divorce: A Guide to Canadian Family Law (2nd ed.), by Michael G. Cochrane, John Wiley and Sons Canada Ltd., 1999.

The Canadian Divorce Decisions Workbook: A Planning and Action Guide, by Julien D. Payne et al., McGraw-Hill Ryerson, 1994.

For more than fifty years, Coles Notes have been helping Canadians through high school, college and university...

- **Shakespeare** – all the famous plays explained, scene by scene
- **Shakespeare Total Study Editions** – includes the original play and a plain English version with scene-by-scene synopsis
- **Literature** – over sixty classic novels, from *Animal Farm* to *Wuthering Heights*, explained chapter-by-chapter with overviews by experts in the field
- **Senior Math** – six books from grade 11 topics to Calculus
- **Senior Science** – Physics, Chemistry, Biology
- **Reference** – from Senior English Essays to French Grammar
- **and still more titles** – *Canadian Law, Senior Accounting, American History, Economics, Advanced Spanish.*

Now our <u>new</u> Coles Notes will help you through the rest of life...

- **Business** – from *How to Write a Great Résumé* to *Start Your Own Small Business*, these books cover the field
- **Personal Finance** – covering stocks, mutual funds, real estate and many other topics to help manage your finances
- **Phrase Books** – seven language books for travellers, including Spanish, French, German and Japanese
- **Lifestyle** – over thirty titles covering gardening, sports and entertainment from *Better Golf* to *Speed Reading*
- **Parenting** – from *The First Year* to *Basketball for Kids*
- **Medical topics** – *Prostate Cancer, Breast Cancer, Thyroid Problems,* with many more to come.

Reliable, economical, authoritative information for Canadians ... Coles Notes

Coles Notes are available at ...

NOTES & UPDATES

NOTES & UPDATES